Over the past ten years the County of Saratoga has grown over 17 percent, making it one of the fastest growing counties in New York State. Our City of Saratoga Springs has been the leading lady in this performance, attracting new people and new companies to a life styled on a wonderful combination of rural charm and urban sophistication.

Our institutions are among the very best of their kind in the nation, from Skidmore College to the Saratoga Thoroughbred Track, from the National Museum of Racing to the National Museum of Dance, from the Saratoga Performing Arts Center to the Saratoga Springs City Center. Add to this our growing industrial base, service sector, and retail centers and we have a combination which properly nurtured should last us well into the beginning of the next century.

Standing in the winner's circle it is all too easy to forget those who led us to the gate. This retrospective is important because it will help us to remember those people and perhaps help us to face the many challenges ahead with the same vision and strength of character as they did.

Senator Brackett, the founder of The Adirondack Trust Company, wrote a letter in 1916 to the Board of Directors who would be in office in the year 2016. In part he exhorted that future board to make sure that the bank ". . . is managed not only for the proper purpose of making money for its stockholders, but also for the development of the community where it is located and to be an example of high dealing to all who come in contact with it." Those sentiments are still the guiding ones for the management of this company. We are proud to present this collection to you and proud to be a part of this great community.

Charles V. Wait
President

THE
DONNING COMPANY
PUBLISHERS

GEORGE S. BOLSTER'S
SARATOGA

SPRINGS

CHRIS CAROLA · BEVERLEY MASTRIANNI · MICHAEL L. NOONAN

The Donning Company/Publishers,
184 Business Park Drive
Suite 106
Virginia Beach, Virginia 23462

Edited by Elizabeth B. Bobbitt
Richard A. Horwege, Senior Editor
Design by L. J. Wiley
Debra Y. Quesnel, Project Manager

Library of Congress Cataloging in Publication Data:

Bolster, George S., d. 1989.
        [Saratoga Springs]
        George S. Bolster's Saratoga Springs/Chris Carola, Beverley Mastrianni,
    Michael L. Noonan.
                p. cm.
        Includes bibliographical references and index.
        ISBN 0-89865-805-5
        1. Saratoga Springs (N. Y.) —Description—Views. 2. Saratoga Springs (N. Y.)—
        Social life and customs—Pictorial works.
        I. Carola, Chris, 1959-   . IV. Title, V. Title: Saratoga Springs.
        F129.S3B65 1990   90-41680
        974.7'48—dc20   CIP

Printed in the United States of America

C O N T E N T S

ADWAY
U.S. HOTEL
RATOGA
SPRINGS

66.

P R E F A C E

George Bolster would have liked this book. When we first began selecting photographs, he had many favorites. Mainly they were of working people, denizens of the city that he loved. He had hundreds of stories about them, stories that made them come alive, stories that he told with great humor and vivacity even while struggling for breath in his final battle with emphysema.

The book would have been richer if George had been able to participate longer. He died on April 11, 1989, when only a few selections had been made. It would have been richer if we could have transcribed dozens of his stories and collected memories from other long-time residents of Saratoga Springs. But that will come later. What we decided to do was show the city through the eyes of the photographers who are represented in the George S. Bolster Collection. Their cameras captured the heartbeat of the city. The three hundred selected photographs celebrate the people of Saratoga Springs. They are a small sample of the thousands that are yet to be printed. We wanted this to be our city's first "family album."

When the book was first proposed, George was wary. History was alive for him. He wanted a vital text that would touch on some of the interesting and important developments that shaped Saratoga Springs in this century: the wars, Prohibition, the Great Depression, gambling and the changing social scene. The text and the pictures not only touch on many of those areas but will be the basis of future research projects that will use the vivid images in this incomparable photographic collection.

When I first began cataloguing this collection with George Bolster in the early 1980s, it was more time consuming than I anticipated. When I began research-ing three hundred photographs for this book, it took more time than I ever dreamed would be necessary.

7

Each photograph told a lengthy story. Finally, we had to stop and edit.

My thanks to all those who participated. Without Charles Wait and the Adirondack Trust Company the book would not have been published. Without the guidance and support of Willard E. "Bill" Grande the printing of the photographs would not have proceeded and without Martha Stonequist, our city historian who proofread, added information and commiserated, the project would have seemed overwhelming. Thanks to Michael L. Noonan, George's assistant for eighteen years who proved invaluable in our research and whose sensitive printing of these photographs always seems to capture George's spirit. Indeed, George once said of Michael, "Nobody north of New York City can handle a darkroom like Mike can." Thanks to Chris Carola for a lively text. And thanks to Wally Alleridice and the Photographic Committee of the Historical Society of Saratoga Springs. All profits from the sale of this book will go toward Historical Society projects, which include the printing and care of the George S. Bolster Collection.

Beverley Mastrianni April 1990

122987, Michael L. Noonan, Photographer, 1987
The current Adirondack Trust Company building was designed by Alfred Hopkins, an architect from New York City, and is an anchor building on the southwest corner of Church Street and Broadway, Saratoga Spring's most important intersection.

ACKNOWLEDGMENTS

We would like to extend our deepest appreciation to the following people who so willingly gave us their time and knowledge so that this book could be made: John Eckert, Norman Fox, Sophie Goldstein, Douglass "Tim" Mabee, Donald Mercer, Floyd McMillian, David Nestle, Leo Roohan, James Schneider, Harry Snyder, Elaine Mann, Michael Sweeney, Al Braim and Anne Magovern.

Special thanks go to Jean Stamm and Ellen de Lalla of the Saratoga Springs Public Library for the use of its Saratoga Room and the valuable resources it contains; to Florence Harshe, Leslie Shaw, Mary Stewart and Robert Yates, the original members of the Photographic Committee of the Historical Society of Saratoga Springs; and to Donald M. Carola for his computer expertise.

Beverley Mastrianni
Chris Carola
Michael L. Noonan

9945/A, Photographer unknown, circa 1855
    This is the oldest photographic image found in the George S. Bolster Collection. It was taken looking north on Broadway from the entrance to Congress Park. On the left was the Stanwyx House which later became Dr. Bedortha's Sanitorium. It burned in 1864.

In 1915 a trolley station was built on the site. This station later became the Drink Hall and is now the Urban Cultural Park Visitor's Center. To the north of the Stanwyx House was Union Hall which grew into the famous Grand Union Hotel. There is a

shopping center there today.
On the right was the original Congress Hall which stood on land that is now part of Congress Park. This area is currently occupied by the library and the Spencer Trask Memorial (the Spirit of Life).

George S. Bolster and His Collection

PHOTOGRAPHERS

"You handle Saratoga, kid,
I'll believe you can handle anything."
—*Billy Bathgate*
by E.L. Doctorow

Shortly before he died in 1989, the 150th anniversary of photography's official coming out party, George Bolster was asked why he bothered to save all those negatives and prints, the ones that came close to inglorious ends in some garbage can but found a home in every cabinet and drawer in his below-street-level studio at the head of Phila Street.

George's reply: "It was history that was being thrown away." His tone was incredulous, as if he couldn't believe anyone would even consider throwing away a link to the past. People don't toss out their birth certificates or discard the family Bible. Why abandon something which reveals as much of who we are or where we come from as any official document or family keepsake? That was George's way of thinking, and it's the reason we have this collection.

In a sense, George could be called the man who "saved" Saratoga Springs. Granted, he didn't prostrate himself before a bulldozer, didn't sign any petitions and didn't fire off any angry letters to the editor to save some doomed building. In fact, George

Bolster didn't keep one brick from falling that wasn't already destined to tumble before the wrecker's ball. A devil's advocate might venture to say that all George Bolster did was save some old photographs from the scrap heap, pictures of other people's dead relatives, prints of race horses long since entombed in the memories of old gamblers, heavy glass-plate negatives with their ghostly images of architectural behemoths so overscale as to be nearly mythical.

As it turned out, what George saved was our past, captured in tens of thousands of images. And after more than one hundred years of progress and changes, it's the images that remain, that give us a link to what we are and who we were, how Saratoga Springs became what it was and how it could be.

A priceless legacy can be traced through George Bolster's collection of photographs. It encompasses Saratoga Springs history from the 1850s, when the town was establishing itself as the "Queen of the Spas," through the 1950s and 1960s, when the grand dame of high society had slipped a bit, propped up by a reputation earned in younger days and slowly losing its jewels to what writer and native son Frank Sullivan called "the fell hand of Progress."

Indeed, most of the landmarks of a bygone era — the Grand Union, the United States, the lake houses, and George's beloved Worden Hotel — can only be resurrected in memory and, thanks to George, on black-and-white prints that give us a glimpse of how it was when our grandfathers were young.

George S. Bolster was born in 1913, the year Saratoga's famous race track was reopened after a two-year hiatus imposed by reformers bent on ridding society of gamblers and bookmakers. But a loophole was found in the legislation that closed New York's tracks, and the Queen of Spas was once again home to the Sport of Kings and her vassals and servants, the most notable being the bookies who arrived each summer on a train dubbed the Cavanaugh Special. Despite reaching the end of its Golden Age, Saratoga Springs wasn't quite ready for retirement in 1913, as some believed. There was still a lot of life left in the dowager queen which was about to embark on a new era of glittering decline, restless slumber and finally, a rebirth — thanks in part to the efforts to honor Saratoga's past glories by saving its remnants, a task given substance and

purpose by what we see in the Bolster Collection.

The Saratoga of George Bolster's youth was a time when horse-drawn carriages still outnumbered automobiles, when barnstormers barrel-rolled over the city and landed at Pitney's farm, attracting posses of wide-eyed boys lugging pails of water to the pilots in the hopes of earning a ride in the most wondrous machines of the era. It was a time of Prohibition and gangsters, crooked politicians and horse rooms and gambling, always the gambling. And, except for what Frank Sullivan referred to as the occasional "moral spasm" of reform, Saratogians embraced it all with unhesitating enthusiasm. Noting that the French missionary and explorer St. Issac Jogues was believed to have passed through what later became Saratoga Springs in the 1640s, Sullivan wrote that "since his visit, saints have been in a minority among the guests."

The town (Saratoga didn't incorporate itself as a city until 1915) was much the same in 1920 as it was when Sullivan was a boy at the turn of the century, its streets lined and shaded by towering elms and chestnut trees (most of which later became casualties to blight, both the manmade and nature-born variety, and whose passing was particularly hard on old-timers such as Sullivan). In describing his High Street neighborhood near the race track, Sullivan wrote: "In winter it was as remote and snowbound as one of Willa Cather's prairie hamlets. In summer it was verdant but dusty, except when washed by rain or when the village sprinkling cart, an equipage second in fascination only to a circus calliope, deigned to squirt its way along it, with an admiring escort of youth in its wake."

As a boy, George was instilled with a love of local history by his grandfather, John C. Bolster, a railroad man with a wealth of stories about Saratoga. As a young man working in Saratoga's hotels, George heard yet more Spa lore, as he was surrounded by the characters and events that attracted such writers as Ring Lardner and Damon Runyon.

So, with an appreciation of Spa history and a keen eye for the characters that made Saratoga Springs what it was, George started saving old photographs, accepted what was given and rescued images that otherwise would have been shattered on trash heaps or doomed to fade away, forgotten

80-113, Photographer unknown, circa 1865

Behind the throng at the Star Spring, on the left-hand side of the photograph, was a wagon with either "Houghton" or "Naughton" written on it. There is no record of a photographer by this name who had a business in Saratoga Springs. He was probably one of the many photographers who traveled from place to place during the early years of photography, setting up briefly to photograph groups, make portraits and take stereo views.

The Star Spring was a favorite watering place that was located on what is now High Rock Avenue between High Rock Spring and the former textile mill.

in attics crammed with family memorabilia.

The photographs represent the work of scores of photographers, from the first daguerreotypists to ply their trade at the Spa to the gypsy photographers who lugged their Speed Graphics around town as they captured on film the images that came to define Saratoga: a place where the high and mighty and the rich and the famous kept themselves busy with the serious art of spending money.

Others came to Saratoga who were not so high and mighty, whose riches and fame were not based on someone else's honest labor but on their own soiled schemes. They too are immortalized on glass plates and film, as are the Saratoga natives, a curious species torn between the big-city hustlers and monied aristocrats they must embrace to survive and the small-town principles they have struggled to cling to since Gideon Putnam welcomed his first guest. The daily goings-on in Saratoga Springs, after the horses had headed south, were photographed by such men as Harry Settle, Charles Hutchins and others who were George's predecessors and contemporaries, partners and competitors, friends and enemies. And, of course, there are the photos George took himself, the portraits that were his specialty, and the stills of summer stock productions at the Spa Little Theater that endeared him to such celebrities as Groucho Marx.

The photographers who worked the Spa were a small herd, though not a close-knit one. The competition among the established photographers in town was fierce. "It was cut-throat," George said. "You'd find one or two established people at a spot, but the rest were all hustlers, including me." The seasonal guys, however, the ones from the out-of-town newspapers covering the races, tended to be a helpful and friendly lot. After a day's shooting at the track, many

82-09/6, Photographer unknown, circa 1880

An early, unidentified photographer set up a table and cameras beside the Washington Spring Pavilion. This picturesque springhouse, (not to be confused with the Washington Bath in the Spa State Park) was located next to the Clarendon Hotel on the site that is currently the Catholic Central High School on south Broadway.

of them would retreat across Union Avenue to one of several favorite bars. One day over a few drinks George was admiring a fellow's Speed Graphic, at that time the camera of choice for any newspaper photographer worthy of the title. George mentioned that he was in need of a new camera, but lamented he couldn't afford a new Speed Graphic. Soon word got out among their circle: "Bolster needs a camera." One of them took it upon himself to procure a camera for his fellow brother of the lens. Soon this photographer, who worked for one of the New York City tabloids, showed up at George's doorstep with a Speed Graphic. George was told he could have the camera and its handmade leather bag for three hundred dollars. Considering himself the luckiest man on earth for getting a thousand dollar camera for less than half the going rate, George paid the man. Later that same August, while George was in the winner's circle waiting to make a shot, another photographer approached him and asked, "Where's so-and-so?"

"He's not here," George said.

"Whataya mean? There's his bag," the photographer said, pointing to where George had set down the handmade leather bag he recently acquired. It was then that he realized he was the owner of hot property, thanks to his larcenous benefactor, who, when last seen leaving town at the meet's conclusion, smiled and waved as George shook a fist in his direction and muttered curses at the "crazy Irishman" under his breath.

More than a hundred years before, a different kind of photographer first appeared at the Spa. In 1839, a Frenchman named Louis Jacques Mande Daguerre announced to the world a chemical process whereby images could be fixed onto polished plates of silver. Photography was born.

Within weeks the process known as daguerreotype reached American shores, where it caused a sensation. Edgar Allan Poe called it, "the most extraordinary triumph of modern science." A thriving industry in daguerreotypes was in place in just a few years. More than four hundred thousand daguerreotypes

71-103/1, Photographer unknown, 1907.

Beyond the arch, temporarily built across Broadway for an encampment of the Grand Army of the Republic in 1907, was the photographic shop of E. A. Record. It was on the third floor of the First National Bank Building at the southeast corner of Broadway and Phila Street. Before Record had his studio there the space was home to the Saratogian.

The Grand Army of the Republic Encampment was a national convention to commemorate the anniversary of the Civil War. Saratoga Springs vied with Atlantic City for the convention. About seventy-five to one hundred thousand people attended. Every hotel was booked as were private homes and boarding houses throughout the area.

were made in Massachusetts in the year ending June 1, 1855, at a time when the state's population was barely one million.

By 1841 there were at least three daguerreotype businesses in Saratoga Springs. Two of the first, listed in an ad in the *Saratoga Whip* as J. Shaw and H.P. Hill, announced their opening in March 1841: "Shaw & Co. will open accommodations for taking portraits by daguerreotype process." Another, John Sawin, Jr., advertised "Daguerreotype rooms in Temperance Hotel."

By 1853, one businessman located near the town's Post Office was touting himself as "one of the oldest daguerreotypes in (the) Union," while another boasted of having "secured an extra whole-sized camera made expressly for Daguerre (that) is one of the best instruments in the country."

But by the 1860s, the Daguerre process that so astonished the world two decades before was now obsolete, replaced by positive-negative photography

that used glass plates dipped into a solution of silver nitrate and exposed in the camera while still wet. This "wet-plate" process had to be done quickly and required photographers to have their darkrooms close by. Some photographers took to wagons, transporting their whole operations to the springs about town, where visitors posed for group or family photos in front of such popular Spa landmarks as the Star Spring, Congress Spring or Washington Spring.

By the 1870s, there were more than three dozen photographers doing business in Saratoga, nearly all of them situated along Broadway in order to be near the hotels filled with seasonal visitors. Business was brisk in the selling of carte-de-visites, small pictures mounted on cards, and stereographs, two photographs mounted side-by-side and viewed through a hand-held lens for a three-dimensional effect.

In the 1880s a dry-plate process was commercialized that made it possible for people to take their own pictures, thus opening photography to amateurs and

15

3229, H.B. Settle, Photographer, 1915

Occasionally Harry B. Settle and J. S. Wooley went on photographic "shoots" together. Settle took this picture. It is unlikely that he would have left his own equipment in the photograph, so one of the men on the bench may be Wooley.

Hathorn No. 3 was discovered in 1905. It is one of the strongest of the saline waters in Saratoga Springs and is noted for its cathartic properties.

setting the stage for George Eastman. Eastman was a dry-plate maker who introduced his Kodak camera to the world in 1888. A Kodak camera cost twenty-five dollars and came loaded with one hundred negatives. After exposing all the negatives, the camera was sent back to Kodak where prints were made, the camera reloaded and the whole package sent back to the owner.

While the Kodak camera popularized amateur photography, the professional photographer still had plenty of work, especially in Saratoga Springs, where men like Thomas J. Arnold, William Baker, Edgar and Fred Doubleday, Harrison Epler and Thomas Magovern operated through the 1890s and into the early 1900s.

Photography businesses in Saratoga Springs then and in later years often merged with other established firms, or split up to join partnerships with newer photographers, until the work of one man would wind up in the hands of another through business deals and other means. Emerson A. Record had a partnership with Baker at several Broadway locations from 1872 until 1882. Baker bought Record's interest in the business in 1883, and Record and Epler opened shop together at 360 Broadway that same year. Epler and Arnold later bought out Record's business, while Record's original partner, Baker, teamed with Magovern from 1891 until 1903 at 446 Broadway.

By 1903, Magovern was advertising his possession of "all negatives made by the old firm of Baker & Record and of W.H. Baker, over 50,000 negatives, covering over 20 years."

Magovern continued to work mostly on Broadway until the late 1930s, a time when a young amateur

16

photographer named George S. Bolster was taking candid snapshots of the regulars at the bar of the Worden Hotel. George, a desk clerk at the Worden, had gained an education in real life by working and hanging around Saratoga's many hotels. The experience, he would later say, was what made him into a well-known cynic. After encountering the characters frequenting Saratoga Springs in the 1920s and 1930s, including politicians and other con men, George found it hard to believe much of what other people professed to be the gospel truth.

George's cynicism may have been hereditary. His mother Caroline found it hard to believe her 15-year-old son when one day he came home from his job as a bellhop at the Saratoga Inn with sixty-five dollars in his pocket, a princely sum at the time for such a young lad, even in Saratoga. George tried to tell her how the gangster Arnold Rothstein (owner of the Brook Casino until he sold it in the early 1920s) pushed a pile of money at him when George delivered an order of spring water to Rothstein's room. Rothstein, in the midst of a card game, said to the boy: "How much do I owe ya, kid?"

Before George could answer, Rothestein pushed the game's entire pot toward him, saying, "See if ya got enough there, kid." Later George counted the money: sixty-five dollars, about sixty-four dollars above the going rate for spring water. When he turned the money over to his mother, as he always did with his earnings, he was met with a cold stare. She sat him down on the edge of his bed and asked, "Where did you get this? Did you steal it? Are you gambling?"

George kept repeating the story of Rothstein and the card game, but his mother didn't believe him. Not long after the incident, Rothstein, the man who fixed the 1919 World Series in what became known as the "Black Sox" Series, was killed in a New York City hotel suite, shot dead in the middle of a card game.

Years later, after his mother had died, George's sister gave him the notebook his mother used to keep track of all his earnings. Next to the date of the Rothstein tip she had written the number sixty-five, and next to that, a large question mark.

In the 1930s, when George began working at the Worden, his wife Helen gave him a small English-made camera that he could fold up and put into his

72-67/8, Photographer unknown, circa 1915.

C. C. Cook "Cookie" was a famous photographer whose career lasted from approximately 1885 to the 1930s. He was a good friend of Harry Settle.

According to track lore the steeplechase jockeys despised him because of his ability to capture their spills. His talent was amazing because there was no fast film at that time and the image of his large format camera was upside down and backwards.

His talent for printing three-scene montages of a race was also legendary. He would show the start, the finish and the winning circle. Unfortunately most of his photographs were not documented as to place and time. Many of them are in the Keeneland-Cook archives.

jacket pocket. With the camera he snapped pictures in the Worden lobby and bar. Working as a desk clerk at the hotel provided a different education than the one taught in schools. "It introduced me to facets of life I never knew about," he would say in later years. As a U.S. Navy radarman during World War II, George took pictures of the daily life aboard a salvage ship, a breech of wartime security regulations that could have landed him in the brig.

George's interest in photography grew out of his natural ability to draw. Art was his first love, and he spent his idle moments at the Worden sketching polo or racing scenes on the back of racing entry cards or any other blank paper he could get his hands on. He took his first pictures when he was ten, making his own box camera and snapping pictures of neighbor-

72-67/1, C. C. Cook, Photographer, circa 1907
   This was a typical photograph by C. C. Cook showing a steeple-chase spill. The horse and jockey are not identified.

hood kids and dogs. An uncle who was friends with Settle often took George to Settle's studio on the corner of Phila and Putnam streets. Settle worked in Saratoga Springs for more than sixty years, forty of them at the Putnam Street location. He later moved to 1 Phila Street, where George eventually wound up with Charles Hutchins, who had worked with Settle before taking over the business in 1956.

Over the years Settle took a large number of glass-plate negatives. When Settle moved up the street to 1 Phila in 1941, crates filled with the glass negatives were slid down the stairs by the movers, breaking many images of Saratoga's past. Many others survived the move, and Hutchins got them in the mid-1950s under the terms of Settle's will.

George and Hutchins formed a partnership in the late 1950s, when they purchased the business and equipment owned by Joe Deuel, who owned a studio located in the top floor of the building at 360 Broad-

way. The studio had been home to a long line of photographers, from Epler and Arnold in the 1880s to Gustave Lorey, who worked there from 1915 to 1946.

In 1958, George began working out of 1 Phila Street. He had been running his businesses out of his home on Walton Street since his discharge from the Navy. In 1966, a year after Hutchins' death, he took over the Hutchins business on Phila Street. Six years earlier, George had built a portrait studio out of the shop's old "Acme News" darkroom formerly used by wire service photographers during August. Already some several thousand images were stored in the studio in gray metal filing cabinets. As the years went by and people in town became aware of George's interest in old Saratoga photographs, the collection grew to number in the tens of thousands.

Putting a price tag on a collection such as this is difficult; the monetary value of a hundred-year-old negative of a hotel torn down forty-five years ago is

77-45/105, Photographer J. B. Gurtler, 1932
The Gustave Lorey studio was above the Van Voast and Leonard Insurance agency at 360 Broadway. This photograph shows the skylight that was added to the original building in 1888 so that the space could be used for natural light photographic portraits. This space was home to other photographers at different times: Record, Arnold, Epler, and Baker.

negotiable. The historic value is not negotiable. Oliver Jensen, writing on the use of old photographs as historical tools, said in *American Heritage* (a magazine he helped establish) that photographs have the "singular power to sum things up." They add detail and atmosphere to history, Jensen wrote, and therefore an understanding of the photograph's subject can be reached that otherwise might be missed within words.

Perhaps no photograph in the Bolster Collection so upholds this theory as the one showing attorneys James A. Leary and Walter Fullerton. Through parts of six decades the law firm of Leary and Fullerton was one of the most successful practices in northeastern New York State. Leary was a driven, no-nonsense man whose whole life centered around his work, whether trying a case against a major railroad or running the Saratoga County Republican Party, on which he held a tight grip for more than thirty years. Fullerton kept to the background and never delved into politics the way Leary did. While Leary was the firm's trial lawyer, Fullerton was the book man. He had a bear trap of a mind, one that could instantly recall cases and their outcomes and in which volumes to find them. Thus a picture of the two young lawyers thought to have been taken by Harry Settle circa 1910, gives us a hint of who these men were. Leary, tight-lipped and glaring at the camera, sits behind his desk, pen in hand, ready to get back to work as soon as the photographer ends this intrusion into his work day. Fullerton, recently out of law school, holds an open book. He stands behind and to the side of Leary, a deferential position and a concession to his partner's superior abilities. The photograph shows more of the

firm's spartan office than of the partners, as if the photographer did not want to get too close to the subjects, especially Leary. Though he did plenty of business for Leary and Fullerton, mostly taking photographs of accident scenes for negligence cases, in this particular picture Settle seems to imply that it is best to keep one's distance from Leary.

There was good reason to be wary of Leary. Saratoga Springs was not a typical American small town. Few places with a permanent population of thirteen thousand, a figure that remained a benchmark until 1950, possessed what Saratoga had to offer. None had the race track and its caliber of racing, and few had the concentration of gambling and top-notch entertainers featured at the casinos and lake houses. All that money and the power it provided were controlled by a handful of men who ran Saratoga Springs and the county with little regard for outside interference, and no one held more power over more years than James A. Leary.

Soon after the investigations into corruption and organized crime in Saratoga ended in the early 1950s, Leary was out of the political game. A seventy-two-year-old lawyer who had held sway over the county Republican party since the 1920s, Leary was acquitted in 1953 on charges of perjury and conspiracy to obstruct justice. It didn't matter. The ordeal of having his business and political dealings dragged out for all to see took something out of him.

The casinos and lake houses, where the top entertainers of the day performed out front and the roulette wheel held court out back, were rackets run by the mob. But the gangsters couldn't roll a die or deal a card without the approval of Leary, whose Republi-

8878/1 detail, H. B. Settle, Photographer, 1938

Thomas F. Magovern, photographer, leaned on the building and posed for his picture outside his place of business at 338 Broadway. He had his studio at that address from 1920 to 1939. Magovern was in the photographic business at different addresses from the 1890s, first in the firm of Magovern and Baker.

The photograph was taken looking north on Broadway towards Phila Street. In the foreground was the popular Colonial Restaurant, owned at that time by Quinn and Sullivan. Walter's Ice Cream was another popular spot. Walter's was originally located in the Saratoga National Bank Building. Ice cream was made in the basement that became George Bolster's dark room. On damp days the floor is still slippery from the ingredients used in the ice cream.

A sign on the tree said "library" and pointed to the door next to the Colonial Restaurant entrance. This sign referred to the Athenaeum, a library and reading room on the second floor.

can party controlled the county district attorney's office and the sheriff's department, and Dr. Arthur J. Leonard, a Democrat whose elected position as commissioner of public safety of Saratoga Springs gave him control over the city police force.

But the investigations put an end to all that, initially causing outrage among the locals who for years had lived and worked off the business gambling brought to town. Gambling was virtually considered a birthright in Saratoga, where it had thrived in one form or another for more than one hundred years. It was as much a part of the social and economic fabric as the springs and grand balls of the previous era. The locations of the horse rooms, where bets were placed on races out back while a more-or-less legitimate business was conducted out front, were known to virtually every man, woman, and child. But the investigations — beginning with Sen. Estes Kefauver's federal probe in 1951 into organized crime and followed by Gov. Thomas Dewey's own politically inspired crusade — for the most part put illegal gambling out of business, a fact resented for years by Saratoga's citizenry. The town kept its legal betting on horses but other forms of gambling, for years illegal but conveniently overlooked in Saratoga, were no longer tolerated, a situation that caught Frank Sullivan's eye as being a "peculiar moral straddle."

Leary died on the evening of October 18, 1963. He died as he had lived most of his life, alone. He was found sitting in a chair in his mansion on North Broadway. With the passing of Leary and Fullerton, who died the previous June, "an era has come to an

58-239/B, Photographer unknown, 1900

A young Harry B. Settle renovated a building at 37 Putnam Street for his photographic studio. He did business at that address for forty-one years. The building was located on the west side of Putnam between Phila and Spring, where the city parking lot is today.

end," said a *Saratogian* editorial. That era, the newspaper editorialized, was one "of party bosses who met and turned back challenges to their authority." A newspaper obituary noted that Leary had not tried a case in six years and was inactive politically for the last eight years of his life. The man dubbed "The Silver Fox" by the local media once proclaimed that "politics is rotten" and offered a bit of advice: "Never run for elective office." Leary believed so much in what he said that he forbade his employees from running for office. To the end, James A. Leary, a man who left chance to the gamblers who made him rich, knew that it was better to be alone on the inside than surrounded on the outside.

Though his photograph appears just once in this book, Leary's influence in Saratoga Springs during the lifetime of George Bolster and many other Saratogians was substantial. And that lone photo of Leary and Fullerton conveys an image that literally is worth a thousand words.

The famous French painter Henry Matisse said that "photography can provide the most precious documents existing." He said that in 1908, when photography was beginning to overcome its image as a second-class citizen in the eyes of painters and sculptors. George Bolster managed to fill a dual role: as an artist with his portrait work, two examples of which are included in this volume and which highlight his skill as a portraitist, and as a documentarian by his preservation of this wonderful collection, a priceless window to a piece of our history.

1, H. B. Settle, Photographer, Easter Sunday 1900

This was Harry B. Settle's first professional photograph. It was of the Union Wheel Club taken on a five-by-eight-inch glass-plate negative. The negative faded, but the images were saved by his application of retouch fluid. Settle was kneeling in the second row, far left. In his hand was a squeeze bulb that was connected by a relay cord to the camera shutter which was tripped by air pressure from the bulb.

Unnumbered, H. B. Settle, Photographer, circa 1940.

Charles Hutchins (right) worked with Harry B. Settle in the 1940s and inherited the photographic business in 1955. They first worked together at 37 Putnam Street, where this photograph was taken. In 1941 they moved to 1 Phila Street to use a space that had previously been used by a variety of businesses.

50-257/5, Photographer unknown, 1950

The "Acme Boys" took photographs of the racetrack for the Acme News service. Prior to the time the Saratoga Racing Association (later the New York Racing Association) had its own facilities, these photographers developed their negatives and prints in Harry Settle's darkroom. The first wire service photos from Saratoga Springs were sent out from here. Harry Settle was in the foreground of this picture with three members of the Acme team. George S. Bolster turned this part of the darkroom into his portrait studio in 1960. It is now part of Lyrical Ballad Bookstore.

86-27, Michael L. Noonan, Photograher, 1986

On this plaque are the signatures of the photographers who, over the years, came to Saratoga Springs for the racing season and used Harry Settle's darkroom facilities. The plaque was started in the shop at 37 Putnam Street and was moved to 1 Phila when Settle moved his studio in 1941. Some of the most famous names in racing photography are on the list starting with Ed Jackson and C. C. Cook in 1910. The last name is well-known Bob Collianese in 1952.

85-44/8, Michael L. Noonan, Photographer, 1985

George S. Bolster was photographed at the handmade easel in his studio, handcoloring a photograph of the bandstand in Congress Park. Surrounding him were other photographs of old Saratoga Springs. On the counter was an ever present bottle of Saratoga Vichy water.

67-109, George S. Bolster, Photographer, circa 1925

This photograph of John C. Bolster, "Gramp," was taken by a twelve-year-old George S. Bolster. George fondly recalled trips taken with his grandfather to places of historic interest in Saratoga Springs and at Saratoga Battlefield.

George's grandfather instilled in him a love of Saratoga Springs and an ability to spin a good story. Both his grandfather and his father worked on the railroad.

70-133/12, E. A. Record, Photographer, 1888, artwork by George S. Bolster, Christmas card 1988

George and Helen Bolster's annual Christmas card was eagerly awaited each year. It was always made from a photograph in George's collection.

This was their last card. It commemorated the "Blizzard of '88." After that storm, the fire department kept all their equipment moving because the danger of fire was great. In this photograph the hook and ladder sleigh paused on Broadway in front of the United States Hotel.

24

21165, George S. Bolster, Photographer, 1965

George Bolster usually did portraits on commission, but he was fascinated by the face of Henry Molton Lee, a longtime Saratoga Springs resident, and wanted to capture him on film. He invited him into the studio one day and related "I took 40 shots before I got the effect I was looking for . . . . it was not posed, I just snapped as we talked." It was one of his favorite portraits and shows a masterful command of lighting.

61765B/J, George S. Bolster, Photographer, 1965
The Saratogian featured the "Best of Bolster" in an edition on July 4, 1967. In the article, George spoke about this photograph of John Slade. "This was taken for a promotional display but it seemed so well to exemplify all the sterling qualities possible in a man like Mr. Slade, who probably is dean of area attorneys and a fine civic leader . . . . it seemed so symbolic of integrity and leadership."

Much later in his life, George laughingly recalled that Mrs. Slade had requested that the hands be included in the photo. He quoted her, "if you can't do anything else get a picture of those hands. Even if I hated every inch of that man, I would still be in love with his hands."

This marvelous portrait is in the collection of Yaddo.

57-309/B, George S. Bolster, Photographer, 1951
Raymond Calkins, a well known regional painter, did a portrait of Monty Woolley, a well-known actor from Saratoga Springs.

Ray Calkins graduated from Saratoga Springs High and attended art school at the Chicago Art Institute. He painted many scenes of Saratoga Springs and made portraits of people who lived here. This portrait of Monty Woolley is in the collection of Norman Fox.

Unnumbered, George S. Bolster, Photographer and artist, 1952

Christmas Cards made from photographs were very popular in the 1940s and 1950s. George Bolster made a specialty of them and some families had them done on a regular basis. Charles and Phyllis Dake had them done for twenty years. This Christmas card also doubled as a birth announcement for Brad Dake.

A few years ago, Philly had George made up sets of the twenty years of cards as a gift for each of her children.

1420, H. B. Settle, Photographer, 1911

The Saratoga Post Office was built on the northwest corner of Broadway and Church Street in 1911. It had previously been located in Town Hall. There have been post offices in Saratoga Springs since 1802. Early postmasters were also businessmen and post offices were located in their stores. In 1911 the postmaster was W. W. Worden. The Post Office hours were 7:30 to 8 p.m., Sundays from 12 to 1 p.m. and holidays from 11 a.m. to 12 noon and 6:30 to 7:30 p.m. Rates of postage were two cents per ounce, first class.

W10, J. S. Wooley, Photographer, circa 1915

This was the interior of the Post Office in 1915. Today it has been remodeled. The skylight was not covered by the Postal Service when objections were raised by the citizens of Saratoga Springs and Mayor Raymond Watkins in the 1970s. The exterior of the building, which acts as an anchor at the important intersection of Broadway and Church Street in the heart of Saratoga Springs, has been restored.

65-157, Photographer unknown, circa 1880

The Saratoga Springs Police Department in their "bobby-hats" were photographed on the north side of Town Hall.

57-49, Photographer unknown, 1917

The Saratoga Springs Police Force lined up with flags to escort Saratoga's doughboys to the station in this World War I photograph. Identified in the photograph are:
    No. 1 James H. King, Superintendent of Police
    No. 2 Patrolman James J. Cummings
    No. 5 Patrolman Thomas Mahar

10.711, H. B. Settle, Photographer, 1944

During World War II the Saratoga Springs High School had a parade to encourage people to purchase war bonds. In this photograph, the Saratoga Springs Police Force led the marchers south on Broadway past the Worden and the United States hotels.

71-117/2, *Photographer unknown, 1902*

Fires were frequent and devastating in most towns and small cities. Saratoga Springs was no exception. This is the Arcade fire of June 14, 1902. It started in the Theater Saratoga at 7 Phila Street and went through the back of the theater into the Arcade Building which was destroyed. The corner building, home to the Citizen's National Bank, was extensively damaged.

69-60/1, *Photographer unknown, circa 1915*

Horses were being phased out of use and new fire equipment was displayed outside the Central Fire Station built in 1883 at 543 Broadway, currently the Fire House Restaurant. In this photograph, the horses can be seen peeking out from behind the equipment on the left-hand side of the picture. Apparently they were put out to pasture but would respond to the fire bell and arrive at the scene of the fire, often jumping fences to get there before the new vehicles.

6676, H. B. Settle, Photographer, 1930

The Saratoga Springs Fire Department proudly lined up outside their new firehouse at 60 Lake Avenue. It was on the site of the original high school. The school had moved up the street to 124-128 Lake Avenue (now Lake Avenue Elementary).

57-306A/10, George S. Bolster, Photographer, 1957

This was one of Saratoga Spring's devastating fires taken from Putnam Street looking up toward Broadway. This fire consumed seven buildings on the east side of Broadway. Notice the fire alarm telegraph box in the foreground of the photograph. When a fire was spotted, a person would open the box and pull the alarm lever. These boxes were placed in prominent places throughout the city and their locations were listed in the city directory. Often pranksters or children turned in false alarms that were the bane of the fire department.

W89, J. S. Wooley, Photographer, 1907

The caption on the lower left hand corner proclaims "Convention Hall Saratoga Place of Many Notable Gatherings." In this 1907 photograph the Hall was decorated in bunting for the Encampment of the Grand Army of the Republic. On the right was the House of Pansa at Pompeia.

Unnumbered, Charles H. Hutchins, Photographer, circa 1955

The versatile interior of Convention Hall was used for many community activities as well as for conventions. Built in 1893, it could seat five thousand people.

Unnumbered, George S. Bolster, Photographer, 1965

Some of the Saratoga Springs most illustrious buildings were lost to fire. Convention Hall had been used by generations of Saratogians and visitors before it burned in 1965. The YMCA stands on the site today.

The fire started in the Columbian Hotel which was closed and slated for demolition. It was directly across the street on the west side of Broadway. Wind arced the flames across the street igniting the cupolas of Convention Hall. The exterior was brick but the interior was shiplap and burned intensely, destroying the building.

84-41/16, Michael L. Noonan, Photographer, 1984

Mayor Ellsworth Jones, Marylou Whitney, Charles Wait, chairman of the Saratoga Springs City Center Authority, and George F. Perkins celebrated a joyous moment at the opening of the Saratoga Springs City Center.

34

80-138, Photographer unknown, 1931

Franklin Delano and Eleanor Roosevelt were frequent visitors to Saratoga Springs. Here they were at the Saratoga Racecourse with George Bull, president of the Saratoga Racing Association, who was standing beside the open car. In another photograph in the George S. Bolster Collection, Eleanor was shown visiting Skidmore College students.

Franklin Roosevelt was instrumental in reviving the Saratoga Spa. In 1929, when he was governor of New York State, Roosevelt appointed millionaire Bernard Baruch (son of Dr. Simon Baruch who

had worked to evaluate and improve the springs) to head a commission to draft a plan for developing the Saratoga Spa. The following year the legislature appropriated $2,000,000 to finance the Spa and construction began. The final cost was $8,500,000.

The complex opened in the summer of 1935. There were three bathhouses (Roosevelt, Lincoln and Washington); the Hall of Springs; the Gideon Putnam Hotel; a new bottling plant for Geyser, Coesa and Hathorn waters; tennis courts; a golf course and a swimming pool.

77-42, Heisler D'Arrigo, Photographer, Albany, N.Y., 1946

Thomas E. Dewey, governor of New York State, spoke to the New York Auto Dealers Association Golden Jubilee Convention held in Convention Hall, Saratoga Springs in July 1946.

In 1948 Dewey challenged Harry S Truman for the presidency of the United States. Although a heavy favorite in the polls, he lost the election. He remained as governor of New York State and, although he was a Republican, he was not a popular figure in Saratoga Springs. In the spring of 1951, U.S. Sen. Estes Kefauver launched an investigation into organized crime that controlled gambling in Saratoga Springs. Governor Dewey convened a special grand jury to investigate. Saratoga's casinos and gambling houses were closed down.

58.353/4, George S. Bolster, Photographer, 1958

Nelson Rockefeller, on the right, is shown with Saratogian John Nichols. Rockefeller was instrumental in getting the Saratoga Performing Arts Center built in the Spa State Park. On June 30, 1964, he climbed onto the seat of a tractor and plowed up a yard of turf adjoining the Hall of Springs to break ground for the center.

8352, H. B. Settle, Photographer, 1936

Addison (Ad) Mallery was mayor and commissioner of public
affairs in 1936. Here he posed on the steps of City Hall surrounded
by a group of Hopi Indians and other celebrities. None of the other
people in the photograph are identified.

Mallery was born at 3 Waterbury Street and was elected Mayor
twelve times, serving from 1936 to 1960. In a letter he sent to the
city historian's office, Mallery recalled that the Mayor's salary was
five hundred dollars per year, but was raised to a thousand dollars a
year for the last few years he was in office.

63-96/3, Charles H. Hutchins, Photographer, circa 1963

Before service was automated, switchboard operators were an essential element of the New York Telephone Company, a major employer of young women at this time. The company was located on Putnam Street. Operators wore headphones and sat on stools before their boards while supervisors occupied the center area.

81-02, Thomas F. Magovern, Photographer, 1924

The Bench and Bar of Saratoga County in 1924 had many names that played an important role in Saratoga Springs. At the time the only woman in the group was Kathryn H. Starbuck.

Bench and Bar

Saratoga County, New York

68-106, George S. Bolster, Photographer, 1968
   This was the Bench and Bar of Saratoga County in 1968. There are also many prominent names and faces in this group. Members of the Bench and Bar have played important roles in Saratoga Springs history both personally and professionally. This group of photographs is an excellent example of the quality of portraiture done by George S. Bolster.

73-24, Photographer unknown, copyright 1897
Wm. S. Kelly publisher of Saratoga Summer Season
   Adelbert P. Knapp, president, was surrounded by village officials and scenes of Saratoga Springs taken from viewbooks.

3730, H. B. Settle, Photographer, 1917

This was the first City Council under the new city charter in 1917. Shown in the Butler, Kilmer and Corbin law offices at 6 City Hall are (left to right): Public Safety, William Millman; Finance, W. H. Waterbury; Mayor Walter Butler; Public Works, N. Remick Thompson and Accounts, Michael J. Mulqueen.

9574, H. B. Settle, Photographer, 1940

Dr. Arthur Leonard (center) and Dr. Fredrick Ressigue (right) were photographed in conversation with an unidentified person at a reception. One of the most respected surgeons in upper New York State, Dr. Ressigue was also president of the Saratoga National Bank. Dr. Leonard was a physician and surgeon with offices at 563 Broadway. He was also commissioner of public safety and a Democratic politician who, along with his Republican counterpart James Leary, controlled much of what went on in Saratoga County from the late 1930s to the time of the gambling investigations in the 1950s.

40

W81A, J. S. Wooley, Photographer, circa 1910

In this photograph of Town Hall (now City Hall), the bell tower and clock were still in place and the lions guarded the front doors. Town Hall was designed by Cummings and Burt, Troy architects. It opened in 1871 and contained the Post Office (from 1903 to 1911), a theater on the second floor (after 1909), a courtroom on the third floor, all necessary spaces for town officials and a "lock-up."

An addition was built on the east side of the building about 1882 to house the Appellate Division of the Supreme Court and to make room for the Police Department.

In the 1930s the building underwent extensive renovation. The bell and the clock tower were removed because the vibrations had supposedly weakened the tower and the foundations of the building. The wrought-iron fence and the lions were removed. (The lions currently reside in the east and west side recreation fields.) The front entrance and the steps were changed at this time.

6556, H. B. Settle, Photographer, 1930s copy of a 1910 photograph

This is a photograph of James A. Leary (seated) and Walter Fullerton as young lawyers in their law offices in Town Hall. The law firm of Leary and Fullerton was one of the most successful in Saratoga County and one of the most prominent in northern New York.

Desjardins Blacksmith Shop was located at 67 Putnam Street. Boyds 1876 Directory advertised: "Wagon work done. Horses shod with care, neatness and dispatch."

Doomed Trade and Fallen Landmarks

TRANSPORTATION

In 1900, Henry Ford took a newspaper reporter for a ride in one of his new horseless carriages, a piece of machinery called the automobile. As he drove past the shop of a saddle and harness maker, Ford told the reporter, "His trade is doomed."

His prediction, of course, became an American reality in the coming decades, and not just for saddle and harness makers. For nothing had a more dramatic effect on the Saratoga Springs hotel business than the automobile. The journey to Saratoga had always been an ordeal, at its worst arduous and bone-jarring in the days of stagecoaches and carriages, at its best noisy and crowded in the first decade of rail travel, except for the extremely rich, who arrived in their own custom-built train cars. The automobile would change all that as the twentieth century wore on.

The Saratoga season, at first a three-month hiatus that began in early June and stretched into early September, became increasingly shorter. June arrivals necessitated by long journeys via ship, steamboat and coach were pushed back to July thanks to the convenience of the ever-expanding railroads. As more and more cars appeared on America's roads, the roads themselves improved, making it easier to get to the Spa — and, of course, other places — and eventually doing away with season-long stays that had become the pillar of the hotel business.

But before the car put the horse out of the mass transportation business, the railroad delivered the first mortal blow. By 1833, carriages pulled by horses along cast-iron rails gave travelers a taste of things to

72-50, Photographer unknown, circa 1900
    The Hackmen's Association met at the Grand Army Hall on Pavillion Street. "Hackies" drove the carriages in Saratoga Springs.

Information on the negative envelope states that "outsiders" had to pay one hundred dollars per license.

come. One such line ran from Albany to Schenectady and later to Saratoga Springs. But the horse-drawn rail cars offered few advantages over stagecoaches; traveling at an average of nine miles per hour, they were as slow moving, and as cramped as their non-rail competitors. Things changed dramatically, however, when the first steam engine made its maiden journey to Saratoga. Various sources put its arrival as July 2 or 3, 1833. The name of that first steam engine is also in doubt, with some crediting the Fire Fly and others the Davy Crockett as being the first to haul a load of visitors to the growing resort town of Saratoga Springs.

Whichever the case, train travel to the Spa had begun in earnest. The Saratoga & Schenectady Railroad was the second railroad to be built in New York State, a year after the railroad connecting Albany and Schenectady had been constructed. The trains had an immediate impact on the Saratoga season. By the end of the 1833, 12,000 summer visitors came to the Spa, more than double the number that had braved the jolting journey over rutted post roads in the preceding year. During one week in July 1833 alone, 3,550 passengers made the twenty-one-mile trip between Schenectady and Saratoga, a journey that lasted one

hour and forty minutes. People were so excited by this new mode of travel that they left room for nothing else; almost no freight moved over the line in its early years.

Saratoga Springs was already a famous watering place by 1830, having edged ahead in popularity over Ballston Spa, its neighbor and competitor to the south. But the desire to win back lost business, and not just the growing favor of Saratoga, is what led Schenectady businessmen to build a rail link with the springs. In the early 1800s, freight headed west was unloaded from Hudson River barges at Albany and transported by wagon to Schenectady. From there the goods were placed on boats that continued the westward journey on the Mohawk River. The Erie Canal, completed in 1825, took business away from the Mohawk River shippers. Looking for opportunities elsewhere, Schenectady businessmen looked north to Saratoga Springs, a converging place for produce grown on the farms in the surrounding countryside of Saratoga and Washington counties.

Ground was broken for the new Saratoga & Schenectady Railroad on August 20, 1831, and construction began on September 1. By the end of October the railroad's builders were desperate for work-

70-109, Seneca Ray Stoddard, Photographer, 1887

Grand in conception, the Delaware & Hudson Railroad Station occupied the total block between Church and Division streets on Railroad Place (the Price Chopper supermarket and parking lot are there today). It was built in 1871 and replaced a much smaller station.

This station was built in high Victorian style befitting Saratoga Springs. It had a bell tower and clock similar to the ones on Town Hall and the Waterworks. As trains arrived, the bell was rung to signal carriages and porters. Carriages backed into place to receive passengers and luggage, often the "Saratoga Trunks" of visitors who stayed for the season.

The first floor receiving platform was of open construction and there was a restaurant on the second floor.

ers, and advertised in one newspaper that "liberal wages would be paid five hundred additional hands." The railroad was opened for business on July 12, 1832. A section of the line spanning the Kayderosseras Creek in Ballston Spa was incomplete, so passengers were transported from one end of the gap to the other by stagecoaches. With the completion of the new line, Saratoga was now linked to Albany via the Mohawk & Hudson Railroad that connected the state capital with Schenectady. Those wishing to leave behind for a day the political hubbub of the Capitol could depart Albany at 6:30 a.m. and arrive in Saratoga before noon, a four-and-a-half hour journey on the horse-drawn rail carriages.

Saratoga Springs' first train depot was located at the northwest corner of Broadway and Division Street, a convenient location for summer visitors in that they arrived just a few blocks from the major hotels, but one that had its drawbacks once guests realized that the trains arrived and departed virtually under the windows of their rooms. Because of this the depot was later moved one block west to Marvin's Square, now known as Franklin Square.

The Saratoga & Schenectady Railroad eventually became an important line in the Delaware & Hudson Railroad. In the summer, as many as 160 people would fill the twenty-four-foot long train cars for pleasure rides that cost $2.50 for a round trip from Schenectady to Saratoga Springs. Other railroads eventually wound their way to the Adirondacks and Vermont, opening New York's North Country and parts of Vermont to Hudson Valley businessmen in manufacturing centers such as Troy. One railroad, the Adirondack Railroad Company, was formed in 1863

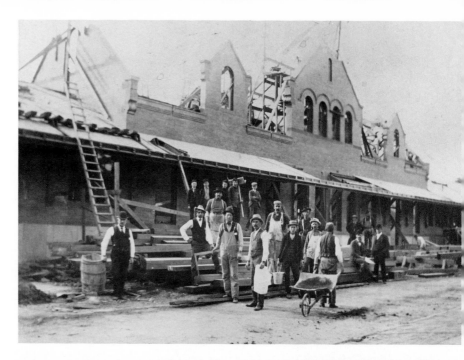

82-91, Photographer unknown, 1900

In 1899 the railroad station burned and by 1900 a new station was being built. The new station was neither as elaborate in ornamentation nor as grand in conception as the previous one but it was more practical because the interior was enclosed to accommodate the growing number of patrons traveling in winter.

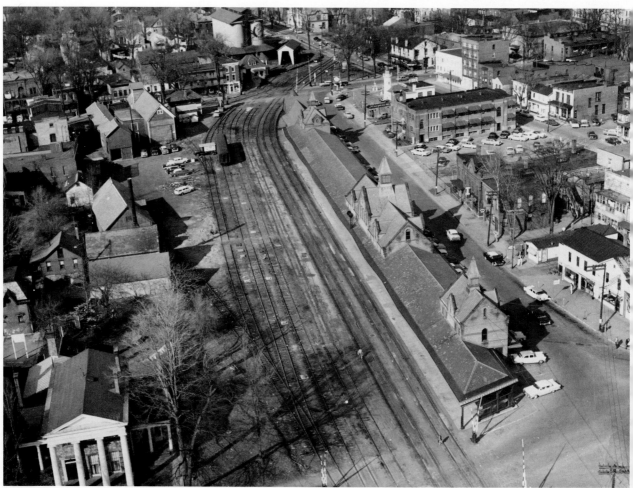

A59-123, George S. Bolster, Photographer, 1959

This aerial photograph gives an excellent overview of the railroad depot and the tracks that were in downtown Saratoga Springs. A spur line in left foreground went to G. F. Blackmer and Son, a wholesale paper and office supplier on Clinton Street, which is still in business, and to the Saratoga Milling and Grain. A second spur ran to the Armour meat packing plant and a third to the Saratoga Coal Company.

The railroad tracks ran behind the station, cut across Woodlawn and Walton streets at an angle, went behind the Central Fire Station on Broadway (now the Old Firehouse Restaurant) and followed what is now the Route 50 arterial out of the city.

In the right foreground were various small businesses on Railroad Place. In front of the station was Millet's Hotel (formerly Sweeny's), a parking lot, the Saratoga County office building (in use today), the Commercial Diner and the Colonial Beacon Esso station. All those buildings, with the exception of the Saratoga County building, all the buildings on Woodlawn Avenue south of Church Street and the depot no longer exist.

5838/5 detail, H. B. Settle, Photographer, 1927

A newly discovered negative gives a clear view of the depot of the Adirondack Railroad which was located on Grand Avenue. Originally this line was constructed as part of a grand plan to open the Adirondacks to tourism, but it was only built as far as North Creek and was used primarily by working people.

The building is currently very deteriorated and its future uncertain. The Saratoga Springs Preservation Foundation has submitted a grant application to rehabilitate the building as housing for the elderly.

for the purpose of building a rail line through the Adirondacks to Sackett's Harbor. It had reached as far as North Creek eight years later, but the remainder of the line was never completed. In the 1870s, the increased popularity of Saratoga Lake with summer visitors and organizers of college rowing regattas led to the construction of a railroad connecting Saratoga Springs with this pristine lake just five miles from the center of town. The line was completed in the early 1880s and eventually reached the towns of Mechanicville and Schuylerville. It later became part of the Boston & Maine and was abandoned in 1950.

In its early years, rail travel was as much a novelty as it was a convenience. Every train arrival was an occasion to gather at the depot and gawk at what one happy traveler called "the new wonder of the age." One observer, William M. Stone, reported: "The cars with horses were a great novelty; but when steam was substituted for horsepower, the astonishment knew no bounds."

The cars, Stone observed, were "spacious and elegant," with three compartments per car, curtained and cushioned for the comfort of each compartment's eight passengers. Among them were the nouveaux riche, people with little or no prominence at home but who could take advantage of the relatively inexpensive train accommodations and travel to Saratoga, where, for a two-dollar-a-day hotel room, they defied all social barriers and mingled with

high-society belles, blue-blooded families and the captains of American industry.

As the nineteenth century wore on and rail travel improved, trains became the main conveyance for people headed for the Spa. The depot on Railroad Place, the site now occupied by a supermarket, became a noisy, bustling mass of humanity with the arrival of each train carrying summer visitors. Carriage and wagon drivers backed their vehicles close to the train platform into predetermined spaces, over which the name of the town's various hotels were painted on signs: United States Hotel, Grand Union Hotel, the Columbian, Congress Hall. The wagons were needed to carry the Saratoga Trunks, a massive hogshead trunk dreaded by porters and packed with everything a fashionable lady of the day would need for a season at the Spa.

Saratoga's train depot was destroyed by fire on March 14, 1843, in a blaze that also claimed a nearby billiard room and bowling alley. Another depot was built, one nearly five times as big as its predecessor. It was 160 feet long by 47 feet wide, with wings containing two tracks on which the trains rode into the depot

63-118/4, Photographer unknown, 1885

Crowds lined the tracks waiting for the funeral train carrying the body of Ulysses Simpson Grant, Union general in the Civil War and eighteenth president of the United States who died on July 23, 1885, at the Drexel Cottage (also called Elberon but now known as Grant's Cottage) on Mount McGregor. The body was brought down from the mountain on the narrow gauge railroad and transferred to the regular line in Saratoga Springs for the trip to Washington, D.C.

2522, Doubleday and Knight, Photographers,
circa 1888

Copy made by H. B. Settle in 1913.
President Harrison and his entourage were
escorted from the Mount McGregor Station
to board the train that would take them to
visit the Balmoral Hotel and the cottage
where President U. S. Grant wrote his
memoirs and died.

This narrow gauge railroad station was at
the corner of what is now North Broadway
and the arterial. The building of the railroad
was begun on Saint Patrick's Day in 1882
and was completed in July of the same year.
It ran from Saratoga Springs to the Balmoral
Hotel on Mount McGregor and on to Lake
George. The hotel burned in a spectacular
fire on November 25, 1897, and the railroad
fell into disuse.

76-122, Photographer unknown, 1921
Passengers boarded trolleys from platforms behind the trolley station at 297 Broadway. Built
in 1915, the station serves today as the Urban Cultural Park Visitor's Center and the City
Historian's Office.

9779/1, H. B. Settle, Photographer, 1941
The interior of the building that was originally the trolley station was known to generations of Saratogians as the "Drink Hall" and was part of the Spa Reservation. People could sit and sample bottled waters of the Hathorn, Coesa and Geyser springs.

9805/C, Photographer unknown, circa 1900
This double decker trolley operated in Saratoga Springs and was photographed on Congress Street beside the Grand Union Hotel. Congress Hall was in the background. "All Aboard for Saratoga Lake" was written below the single deck portion of the trolley. This is the only photograph of a double decker that has been found in the collection at this time. It came into the collection when the Hudson Valley Railroad asked H. B. Settle to copy a photograph of "old cars" in 1941.

through arched doorways. A large cupola gave the ornate structure a height of forty feet. Nearby a brick building contained the machine shop. This depot was replaced in 1871 by another, more elaborate structure on Railroad Place, which also fell victim to fire, one that broke out in the early morning hours of February 9, 1899. High winds in the subzero weather fanned the flames and blew cinders across the street, which resulted in the destruction of Sweeny's Hotel and several other buildings. Another depot was built, one finished in time for the inaugural run of the Saratoga Special in 1901. This train, equipped with cars for dining, smoking and reading, left New York City's Grand Central Station every afternoon and covered the 180 miles to Saratoga Springs in 210 minutes. The New York Central & Hudson River Railroad operated the Saratoga Special from New York to Troy, where the Delaware & Hudson would take over for the final run to the Spa. Saratoga's popularity in the 1880s and 1890s proved to be a boon to the railroads as well. The D&H built another line from Troy to the Spa to handle the increased business. While Saratoga depended heavily on train travel during the summer months, the railroads benefited from a healthy tourist trade. Any disruptions showed up in railroad ledgers. When fires destroyed the United States Hotel in 1865 and Congress Hall in 1866, passenger travel to the Spa suffered so much that the D&H loaned thirteen thousand dollars to the owners of Congress Hall to speed their rebuilding plans.

81-24, Photographer unknown, 1901

This is a photograph of the Hudson Valley Motor Company described in the text of the book.

63, H. B. Settle, Photographer, 1903

In the very newest motorcar, the family of W. H. Chapman prepared for an August outing. Notice the steering column with a horn, the gas lamps and the basket mounted behind to carry provisions. Most of the traffic was horse-drawn so the streets were not yet paved.

599/1, H. B. Settle, Photographer, 1908
H. E. Pettee was the mayor of Saratoga Springs in 1908. He was referred to as "The Mayor with the Bear Behind" by George Bolster.

Over the years, Saratoga's train depots became the place where visitors said goodbye until next year, where soldiers going off to war saw their loved ones for the last time, where generations of Skidmore College women caught the first glimpse of their home for the next four years.

But train travel would steadily give way to automobiles, made affordable by Henry Ford's assembly line manufacturing techniques. Ford turned fifty in 1913, the year George Bolster was born and the year the moving assembly line was introduced at a Ford plant in Highland Park, Michigan. Robert Lacey, in his 1986 biography of Henry Ford, wrote how the automaker spent the summer of 1913 "working on the details of the belts, chutes, and slides which were to revolutionise (sic) the twentieth-century workplace." By 1916 nearly half a million Model T's had been sold. That figure nearly doubled five years later, and through the early 1920s sales for Ford's Model T topped the one million mark every year.

In the early 1900s, there was at least one company building automobiles in Saratoga Springs. Charles Mayhew started the Mayhew Gas Engine Company at 31 Geneva Street. The business was later renamed the Hudson Gas Motor and Vehicle Manufacturing Company, listed in city directories at the same Geneva Street address. Fred Tarrant, whose father William was president of the company in 1901, believed only two cars were built by the company

during its short life. The son said the first car "ran fitfully (and) cracked like a rifle, and could only be driven evenings when most horses were off the streets. The second was improved. It vibrated badly, but it did run and could climb hills."

Mayhew later left town and William Gage took over the chassis of the automobile Mayhew owned. The company was renamed the Gagemobile Company and was listed in the 1905 city directory at 29-31 Excelsior Avenue, formerly Geneva Street. By 1906, the company was out of business.

Thomas Ward is believed to have opened the first garage in the village in the early 1910s, when automobiles were still somewhat of a novelty. By the mid-1920s, Broadway was choked with cars and trucks during the August season. Although the occasional horse-drawn wagon still appeared on city streets, America now traveled on four wheels instead of four legs. As roads went from dirt to hard-top macadam, more of the country became accessible to those who were more or less confined to their towns because transportation was difficult. Improved roads opened up new places to go, even if they were just a few minutes' ride away. This meant more people could reach the Spa, but it also meant other diversions and destinations previously out of reach were now within the common man's realm. It also accelerated the decline of Saratoga's "stately ornaments," as Frank Sullivan wrote of the grand hotels in later years.

72-70, Photographer unknown, circa 1915

American Express employees were photographed at the D.&H. Railroad freight depot off west Circular Street. Standing in the center, (fifth from right) with bow tie and suit was George S. Bolster's father. Both his father and grandfather worked on the railroad. When George was about eight years old, his father was seriously injured in a train accident and died a few years later.

6359, H. B. Settle, Photographer, 1929

It was the barnstorming era and planes would land at "Pitney's Airport" located on West Avenue just south of St. Peter's Cemetery. Boys from town would ride their bicycles out to the airport in order to fetch water or run errands for the pilots, hoping to get a ride in return. In 1932 the airport was listed as the Saratoga Airport, Inc., indicating that air travel was coming of age.

7384, H. B. Settle, Photographer, 1933

Dusenberg and Rolls Royce automobiles were frequently seen on the streets of Saratoga Springs during the season. Prospective owners of the very newest models could see them displayed in the elegant *Crystal Room of the Grand Union Hotel where they were on loan from Ross Ketchum's garage.*

8076, H. B. Settle, Photographer, 1935

Ross Ketchum Company operated a garage and automobile dealership on Broadway north of Convention Hall (it is the building next to the YMCA today). The area in the foreground, where the new owner of a Rolls Royce was being congratulated, was originally part of the back yard of the trolley station where the tracks exited onto Broadway.

8342, H. B. Settle, Photographer, 1936

Bill Ford's distinctive Colonial Esso Servicenter was located on Church Street between Woodlawn and Railroad Place (a Stewart's store is on the location today). Service was excellent. In this photograph one man was pumping gas and another was replacing radiator fluid.

Behind the station was the Commercial Diner which was located on the site that had been occupied by the Commercial Hotel. Behind the diner was the building that, in 1928, was the Griffon Shirt Company and became Isidore Helitzer and Brothers Incorporated in 1930. They were dress manufacturers. By 1935 it was being used by the county of Saratoga. It continues to be used by the county and has recently undergone extensive interior renovation.

HOTELS AND BARS

72-60B, H. B. Settle, Photographer, circa 1925

George Bolster found this negative in a drawer. It was very dusty but he cleaned it off and printed it. He surmised that it was a photograph which H. B. Settle had told him about that was taken from a Ford Tri-Motor Transport plane before World War II.

In this view, Convention Hall was in the foreground. Across from Congress Park was the Grand Union Hotel. Beyond that was the United States Hotel. In between these two giants, and dwarfed by

them, was the American-Adelphi Hotel (now the Rip Van Dam and Adelphi Hotels).

The bell tower and clock were still in place on Town Hall. Behind and to the north of the United States Hotel, on Railroad Place, the long roof line that was the Delaware and Hudson Railroad Station can be seen.

By the 1920s, Saratoga's two majestic jewels, the Grand Union and United States, were already showing their age. Modern conveniences taken for granted at newer hotels were sorely lacking at both places. In George Waller's *Saratoga: Saga Of An Impious Era*, the author writes that the two hotels were "worn and faded and unable to muster between them one room in ten with a private bath, and scarcely more than that with hot running water . . ." The "States," the younger of the pair, turned fifty years old in 1924, the original structure having been destroyed by fire in 1865. The

rebuilt hotel opened in 1874, the same year Alexander T. Stewart, the wealthy New York City dry goods merchant and new owner of the Grand Union, unveiled a rejuvenated version of that hotel after a two-year refurbishing. Prior to that it was known as the Union Hotel, which had its origins in the early 1800s. The writer Henry James, a visitor to the Spa in 1870, referred to the Union and the newly rebuilt Congress Hall as "two monsters which stand facing each other" on opposite sides of Broadway.

The original Congress Hall, built by Gideon Putnam

113, H. B. Settle, Photographer, 1905

The Daily Saratogian announced on the front page June 17, 1905: "The National Eclectic Medical Association, the great organization of physicians of the Eclectic school of the United States are this week being entertained by Saratoga Springs to the number of two hundred or more, with wives and daughters, they began arriving in town last night and continued today. The convention, The Associations thirty-fifth annual, will continue through Thursday . . . ." The group posed in the courtyard of the Grand Union Hotel for this official photograph.

The courtyard was parklike, surrounded by wings of the hotel. The front wing occupied the block from Washington to Congress Street and contained a front and rear piazza, a drawing room, parlors, shops and the office. The wing that extended another city block along Congress Street held the dining room (275 feet long), kitchen and ballroom (82 feet long). The Washington Street side surrounded Bethesda Church. The hotel occupied over seven acres and had over a mile of piazzas.

in 1811, became Saratoga's first great hotel. By 1860 it had a large piazza facing Broadway, 20 feet wide by 251 feet long, and boasted of 296 rooms plus private parlors. In 1859, while Southerners still flocked to the Spa in large numbers, Congress Hall laid claim to having hosted the most guests, 5,399 to the United States' 4,412 and Union Hall's 3,995. One critic of the period wasn't impressed by the piazza or the numbers, referring to the structure as an "immense wooden caravanserai . . . with no pretensions to architecture . . . and built with the sole view of affording the average accommodations of packed herrings to an indefinite number of persons." That same critic went on to describe the small, cramped rooms with furnishings that "resemble those seen in penitentiaries."

Whatever its deficiencies, Congress Hall remained Saratoga's pre-eminent hotel until 1866, the year fire destroyed this grand structure as well as the

Columbian Hotel. Congress Hall was supposed to open for the season that year on May 29, but a fire broke out the night before and destroyed the hotel in an hour. Rebuilt by 1868, the new Congress Hall was even more splendrous, with accommodations for upwards of one thousand people, Broadway frontage measuring 416 feet, and two 300-foot wings extending back to Putnam Street. Its walls were 20 inches thick and hollow in the center, "thus securing great strength and protection from heat in the summer."

But the reincarnation of Congress Hall stood fewer years than its predecessor. In 1913, Congress Hall was torn down, the victim of failing finances and its own huge size; like many of its similar-sized competitors in town, it had to make a large profit in just a few months' time to meet the demands of creditors and banks. That left the Grand Union and United States hotels to share the glory of being the last of the great Broadway hotels. They did so for thirty more years,

12.604, Photographer unknown, 1893

Monty Woolley was an actor and director who grew up in Saratoga Springs. He celebrated his fifth birthday in the ballroom of the Grand Union Hotel where his father was a part owner and manager.

Woolley was teaching in the English Department at Yale when, according to legend, Charles Brackett recommended him for the role of Sheridan Whiteside in "The Man Who Came To Dinner." Charles Brackett was a Hollywood screenwriter and producer who had also grown up in Saratoga Springs. Brackett felt that Woolley was exactly the cantankerous character that was being sought for the play. Woolley gained fame in the role.

Woolley bought a home in Saratoga Springs in 1943 and was seen so frequently in the company of Frank Sullivan and former Mayor Clarence H. Knapp that they were dubbed "The Three Musketeers." Monty Woolley Day was celebrated by the City of Saratoga Springs on August 1, 1949. There was a parade, followed by speeches, lunch at the racetrack with a Monty Woolley race and a banquet.

At the banquet, held in the Grand Union Hotel, a recording was played with readings by his life-long friend Cole Porter. Bette Davis, Ida Lupino, Shirley Temple, "Prince" Michael Romanoff, John Lund, Jimmy Durante and other entertainers also sent greetings. In his remarks at the dinner, Woolley said: "Several years ago we made a grave error. One of our biggest hotels, second only to this hotel in size, through mismanagement or neglect was unable to continue and it was sold for taxes. It was sold to a man whose name I do not even know and it was destroyed. We made a great mistake and I want to warn you as Saratogians not to make that mistake again." (Saratogian August 2, 1949)

The remarks apparently met with general approval and there was enthusiastic applause. The Grand Union Hotel was demolished three years later.

until World War II delivered the coup de grace to the United States Hotel, while its stately neighbor lingered on for a few more years. But for nearly three-quarters of a century, these two massive hotels attracted the world's most powerful men and beautiful women, who during the summer months lined the porches in the day and filled the ballrooms at night with more finery and wealth than was gathered at any one location in the nation. The women were the envy of the western world, although one contemporary, Sophie Sparkle, described them as ". . . those foolish butterflies of fashion." The women held center stage, the men paid for it. "The people who spend the most at Saratoga," she wrote in 1873, "are the old men with young wives."

Years later, a woman who had worked at the Grand Union in her youth told a *Saratogian* reporter that those who stayed at the hotel "were the kings and

52-260, H. B. Settle, Photographer, 1952

The Grand Union Hotel lobby, although somewhat worn, still displayed the elegance of a bygone era. However, the sign on the left, portending things to come, announced the sale of the contents and furnishings. After the last day of racing in 1952, the hotel closed. The contents were auctioned in September and the hotel was razed.

81-44, Michael L. Noonan, Photographer, 1981

This contemporary shopping mall was built on the site of the Grand Union Hotel. Beyond the mall is the side of the Rip Van Dam Hotel. Behind the mall the top portions of Bethesda and the old Methodist Church (now the United Baptist Church) can be seen.

74-46, Record and Epler, Photographers, 1888

On March 11, 1888, a giant blizzard began. Before it was over on March 14, Saratoga Springs had fifty inches of snow, three inches more than any surrounding area. Drifts were piled up to forty feet. In this photograph, three gentlemen in top hats and shovels posed on the top of a snowbank. In the background were the American-Adelphi, the United States and the Worden Hotels. The American-Adelphi *was built in 1840. Although one hotel, the American was run on the American plan and the Adelphi on the European plan. Today they are separate businesses and the only surviving old hotels on Broadway. The American was extensively remodeled and is now called the Rip Van Dam. The Adelphi has been restored and visitors to this hotel can enjoy the flavor of a bygone era.*

queens of society." Jane Trinkle was eighty-three when she visited her former hometown in 1946. The daughter of a mason, Trinkle was a seventeen-year-old girl when she worked at the Grand Union and Congress Hall and later Woodlawn Park, the estate of Judge Henry Hilton (who, as proprietor of the Grand Union, caused a furor when he barred Jews from the hotel in the 1870s). Trinkle could recall every detail of the Grand Union's famed Crystal Room, telling a reporter that it had twenty-four windows with a mirror between each, plus fifty-two windows in the dining room (though the account never mentions the woman's job at the hotel, it is possible she was responsible for cleaning the mirrors and windows, thus accounting for her keen recollection of the details).

"The parlor as it was then called, was a favorite tryst of fashionables seated in the luxuriant furniture," the woman told the reporter.

Inside, the Grand Union and United States operated as though oblivious to the outside world, catering to the rich and powerful like a land-locked *Titanic* and *Lusitania*, and just as doomed. But in the last decades of the 1800s, the hotels had few rivals in the civilized world, and Saratoga Springs was at its grandest. Seneca Ray Stoddard, a writer of travel books who later would gain his greatest fame as a photographer and cartographer of the Adirondacks, wrote in 1881: "Whatever one feels like enjoying, that comes under the head of purchasable pleasure, can generally be had at Saratoga."

59

W66 detail, J. S. Wooley, Photographer, 1907

This was the most popular of the hand-colored photographs done by George S. Bolster. At the time of his death, he had colored 159 copies and two more were in progress.

Broadway teemed with cars, carriages and promenading people. The United States Hotel was on the left hand side. Nothing in this photograph remains today. The United States Hotel came down in 1946. The block of buildings across the street burned in a terrible fire in 1957. Dutch Elm disease destroyed the trees.

W95, J. S. Wooley, Photographer, 1910

In 1874 the United States Hotel opened on the site of the original Eliza Benedict's Guest House which had burned down. It had a 233 foot front facade and numerous cottage suites that extended along the south wing. All the 768 guest rooms had marble washstands and cold running water. Only the suites had private baths. The decor featured carved furniture, flowered carpets and lace curtains.

After the turn of the century, when this photograph was taken, women's clothing was long and elaborate and automobiles were just beginning to replace carriages as the mode of travel.

60

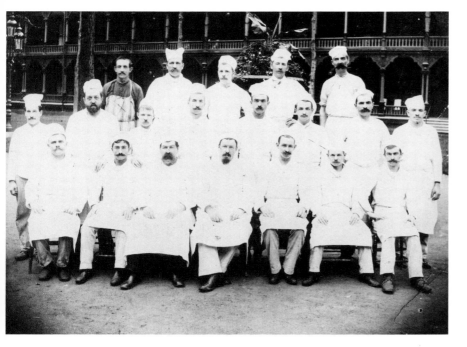

72-218, W. H. Baker, Photographer, 1889

In his book Saratoga-Saga of an Impious Era, George Waller states: "The United States could boast . . . of a superbly appointed drawing room, ballroom and dining room, which could seat 1000 guests, and in the vast cellar was a large wine chamber and a still larger meat chamber. Before the social season Saratoga's farmers would drive herds of cattle and sheep into the cellar, where they would be slaughtered and the meat stored for the kitchen." Three meals a day were served. Mid-afternoon dinner, which often took over two hours, was the main event.

Stoddard, enamored of Saratoga's tree-lined streets that offered a "delightful sense of protection from the summer sun," also sung the praises of Broadway, "of which any city in the world might be proud; a broad, beautiful, elm and maple shaded avenue . . . ."

Saratoga thrived in this era. The race track, begun by gamblers during the Civil War to offer visitors yet another way to part with their money, was a grand success. The springs continued to attract waves of devotees. Culture, wealth and international attention brought to Saratoga a stature well out of proportion to its permanent population of seven thousand. But Saratoga's Golden Age didn't last long into the new century, and with its passing came the beginning of the end for the Grand Union and United States hotels. Gambling reforms that closed the casinos and then the race track in 1911 and 1912 hastened their downfall, as did World War I and later the Great Depression. Gasoline was strictly rationed during World War II, and trains that once transported horses to the Spa were needed for the war effort. As a result, racing was canceled for the 1943, 1944 and 1945 seasons. It was the final setback for the biggest of Saratoga's hotels. The States was razed in 1946 and the Grand Union followed it into history six years later, a devastating one-two punch that took a large bite out of a once grand Broadway.

Saratoga's array of other hotels, many of them situated up and down Broadway like tugboats attending to ocean liners, may have been overshadowed by the vast size and grandeur of the United States and Grand Union, but they nevertheless held an important place in the Spa's history and development as a resort town. By the time George Bolster was born in

1913, there were twenty-seven hotels and more than three dozen boardinghouses listed in the city directory. The latter were known for being a notch above the boardinghouses found in most communities. Seneca Ray Stoddard noted the excellence of Saratoga's boardinghouses in 1881, commenting that they were a cut above those elsewhere because they were not "kept by the butcher's wife, or other keen, heartless business women . . ." Instead, Stoddard wrote, the boardinghouses, like Saratoga's hotels, were ". . . unique in everything, and unapproached in excellence anywhere else."

Of the various hotels in Saratoga Springs' past, some live on only in memory: The Clarendon, the Windsor, the American, the Columbian, the Arlington which later became the Worden, and the many seasonal hostelries that catered to the Jewish summer visitors. Some, like many structures of the period, came to fiery demises in the periodic fires that dot Saratoga's history. Others, like the Grand Union and United States, were spared from fires only to meet a more ignoble end before the wrecker's ball. One of the latter was the Worden Hotel, which stood at the corner of Division and Broadway across from the States for ninety years.

The United States Hotel fire in 1865 also destroyed a number of businesses across Division Street, including a hotel owned by Philip Snyder and named the Marvin House after Thomas J. Marvin, one of two brothers Snyder had borrowed money from to build the hotel. After the fire, proprietors Adam and Don Snyder rebuilt the hotel by the next season. One contemporary guidebook described it as "one of the best constructed hotels in Saratoga and will accom-

74-165, Photographer unknown, circa 1930
   This photograph is a "clip" from the movie Saratoga starring Jean Harlow and Clark Gable. It was given to George S. Bolster by the film crew for his "assistance." Jean Harlow died during the filming so in her last few scenes she was played by a stand-in who was only filmed in one-third profile.

9305/4, H. B. Settle, Photographer, 1939
   Despite all the efforts of the New Deal, ten million people were unemployed in 1939. Saratoga Springs, however, remained an escape valve for thousands who came each summer. These visitors were no longer the elegant socialites who spent the long months of summer at the springs. Now the visitors were the smaller bettors who enjoyed a day at the track, a drink in the bar at the United States Hotel (shown in this photograph) and, possibly, an evening of dinner, entertainment and gambling at one of the lake houses. The elegant dining rooms and ballrooms of the large hotels had fallen into disuse.

8480/1, H. B. Settle, Photographer, 1936
   Gangsters and racketeers were present in Saratoga Springs in the summer, although they were understandably shy about having photographs taken and there are only one or two in the George S. Bolster Collection. The man on the right in this photograph, taken in the Grand Union Hotel bar, was Owney Madden who was reputed to be one of the directors of a syndicate that operated the casinos in Saratoga during August. Other directors included names like "Dutch Schultz," "Lucky" Luciano and "Waxey" Gorden. Luciano presided over the action at the Chicago Club where Arnold Rothstein, owner of the Brook, was a silent partner.

55-283, Photographer unknown, circa 1874
The Grand Central Hotel was located at the southwest corner of Broadway and Congress Street where the Urban Cultural Park Visitor's Center is today. It was built in 1872 and burned in 1874. After this fire, a citywide fire hydrant water system was established. Before this time, water was drawn from the village brook.

modate 300 guests. It is five stories high surmounted by mansard roof and presents a neat and attractive exterior on the fashionable avenue of the town."

The new Marvin House thrived while the owners of the United States, Columbian and Congress Hall hotels rebuilt their establishments, which had all been destroyed by fire. The Snyders ran the hotel into the 1870s, when it was bought and renamed the Arlington. In 1885, the hotel was bought by William W. Worden, who promptly renamed the business. Worden had arrived in Saratoga Springs after the Civil War and ran a lumber business that supplied most of the city's great hotels with sashes, doors and blinds. When his mill burned down, he went into the hotel business. Worden later served as county sheriff and postmaster of Saratoga Springs, then turned the lease to his hotel over to a Joseph Kelly. Three years after Kelly died in 1915, the Worden's lease was assumed by Edward C. Sweeny.

Sweeny and his brother Martin were experienced hoteliers, having operated hotels in New York City, Palm Beach and Saratoga Springs. Edward purchased the Worden in 1921 from the Marvin estate and made improvements to the aging establishment, including installation of plumbing in rooms without hot and cold water.

As one of the few Saratoga hotels to remain open all year, the Worden became a popular spot for locals and visitors alike. The downstairs bar and grill was a favorite meeting spot for famous and not-so-famous alike. Writer Frank Sullivan and actor Monty Woolley, whom Sullivan considered a "carpetbagger" because he moved to Saratoga when three years old, were often to be found at a table, perhaps reciting the bawdiest Shakespearean verses they could muster. One regular customer was a retired dentist who often brought his pet rooster named Mike, who would be set up with a beer at the bar just like a paying customer.

"Oh, characters, good God!" is how George Bolster summed up the regular crowd at the Worden in its heyday. Characters they were, and each seemed to have a nickname: "The Mayor of Antioch," "Choke," "Firpo," "Steamboat," "Chick." Then there was Fritz the dog, owned by Edward Sweeny and so loved by summer guests and townspeople alike that his passing away at age eleven in 1944 warranted a short obituary in the *Saratogian*.

After Sweeny's death, William E. Benton, a former owner of the Grand Union Hotel and Saratoga County Republican party chairman, bought the Worden in August 1945. When Benton died, ownership was passed to a succession of corporations, the second of which renamed the hotel the New Worden Inn. But Saratogians still preferred the old name and continued to call it the Worden. The New Worden

1537/3, H. B. Settle, Photographer, 1912

An early automobile accident at the corner of Circular Street and Broadway was photographed by Harry B. Settle. Apparently the police stopped all traffic until he had photographed the accident from all angles and developed the glass-plate negatives.

Because of this accident, we now have photographs of the buildings that were on these streets. This shot was of Broadway looking north from Circular. On the left was Mrs. Eli Cook's house and then the Everett House (now the Inn at Saratoga). Beyond it was the Huestis annex (the Huestis House was across the street), then the Linwood followed by St. Peter's Church.

On the right was the home of Mrs. Freelove Moon (now the Holiday Inn), the Huestis House (later known as Hotel Gross) and the Windsor Hotel. Beyond that the towers of Convention Hall were faintly visible.

4322, H. B. Settle, Photographer, 1920

The Columbian Hotel was located on the west side of Broadway opposite Convention Hall. It had a kosher dining room and was one of a number of hotels in Saratoga Springs that catered to Jewish visitors.

S30, Photographer unknown, circa 1880

The Windsor Hotel stood approximately where the parking lot and the north section of the Holiday Inn is today. Just beyond the Windsor was the Huestis House. The children were standing in front of a lawn that was between the Windsor and the House of Pansa, a *museum of Pompeian Art. The Community Court Motel now stands on the lawn area. The Windsor was taken down between 1913 and 1914.*

didn't last long under its new name. Fires were to take huge bites out of downtown Saratoga Springs in the 1950s and 1960s, claiming, among others, Convention Hall and nearly a whole block of buildings on Broadway. The Worden narrowly escaped being added to the list when a blaze severely damaged the building in July 1961. Soon afterward, the building was torn down, and a motel was built on the same lot, taking the New Worden as its name.

Broadway had lost yet another landmark. In his last years George Bolster would gladly discuss the

Worden. It held a special place in his memory, for in his early years the Worden was a second home and a different kind of school. "There I learned about life," George said, "and all that goes with it." He also learned how to use a camera, not just to take snapshots, but to preserve a piece of time for when the physical evidence has long faded away, and all that remains are pictures and memories of the Mayor of Antioch, Fritz the dog and Mike the beer-drinking chicken.

S26, Photographer unknown, circa 1880

Heavily patterned carpets and wallpaper, damask chair coverings with lace backs, mirrors, statuary, enormous vases and objects of art were all part of the high Victorian style that welcomed visitors to the Windsor Hotel.

W11, J. S. Wooley, Photographer, circa 1904

In 1811 Gideon Putnam began building the Congress Hall which was located where the library and the Spirit of Life are today. He fell from the scaffolding and died as result of his injuries. Doanda, his wife, and his five sons completed and ran the hotel. The original building was destroyed by fire in 1866. This brick hotel was built on the site by H. H. Hathorn.

The Civil War Monument stood in the center of Broadway. Notice several motorized vehicles as well as two horse-drawn omnibuses on Broadway.

78-21/2, Photographer unknown, circa 1875

Gentlemen at leisure relaxed on the piazza of Congress Hall in this photograph taken for a stereoscopic card. Congress Hall had a number of unique features. There was a promenade, with a view, on top of the hotel that could be reached by an elevator. There was also a bridge across Spring Street that connected it with a building which housed the ballroom (this building is still standing). The ballroom was the scene of extravagant "hops" and social events.

Hathorn Spring No. 1, named for the proprietor of Congress Hall, was discovered during the excavation of the ballroom. One of Saratoga's most popular springs, it can be sampled today at the corner of Spring and Putnam streets.

In 1909 a bill was passed in the New York State legislature creating a State Reservation at Saratoga Springs. It was proposed that the village spend $250,000 to acquire Congress Park and the block immediately adjoining it to make a "great park." By 1913 Congress Hall had been purchased and demolished to accomplish that goal.

4787/A, H. B. Settle, Photographer, 1922

This photograph shows the Saratoga Inn after it had been remodeled by T. J. Flanagan. Originally the building had tall, graceful columns extending three floors above the ground level entrance, much like the facades of the other major hotels. It was first known as the Holden House, then Flanagan's Hotel. After it was remodeled in 1919 it became the Saratoga Inn. George S. Bolster worked at the Saratoga Inn for a number of years.

Today the building is once again changed and is home to Image.

9809, H. B. Settle, Photographer, 1941

Originally built as part of the revitalization of the Saratoga Spa in the 1930s, the Gideon Putnam Hotel was designed by Marcus T. Reynolds of Albany. It was a small hotel at the time with only eighty-seven guest rooms on three floors. The first floor held the lobby, a main dining room and a small dining room for meetings, lounges and writing rooms. At the back of the hotel was a terrace overlooking the new golf course.

Named after Saratoga's premier hotel builder, Gideon Putnam, it was leased for five years by Edward C. Sweeny, proprietor of the New

Worden Hotel. It was to operate on a year-round basis and give preference to Spa patients.

Over the years the hotel has been leased to different proprietors and has had additions and renovations. In 1982 the New York State Office of Parks, Recreation and Historic Preservation commissioned a study of the park. It solicited bids and proposals and selected T/W Recreational Services for a fifteen-year contract to renovate the hotel and the Roosevelt Bath House.

7615/7, H. B. Settle, Photographer, 1934

At the end of World War I, the gambling scene in and around Saratoga Springs changed. Casinos opened in former lake houses with names like Riley's, the Arrowhead, Newman's and Piping Rock. Other clubs opened in Saratoga Springs. Just west of town on Church Street near Locust Grove Road was the most posh casino of all, the Brook, which is shown in this photograph. It was run by Arnold Rothstein. Patrons were required to wear evening clothes and the dining room had a national reputation. Despite Prohibition, liquor flowed freely.

Rothstein had arrived in Saratoga Springs as a young bookmaker in 1904. By the twenties he owned the Brook, a stable of horses, was a silent partner in the Chicago Club (another Saratoga gambling establishment) and had many "investments" in New York City.

He was acquitted of charges of being one of the gamblers who bribed the eight players of the Chicago White Sox to throw the 1919 World Series. By 1928 he was not welcome at the racetrack. His "enforcers" kept people who welched on bets to a minimum, but also made him a figure to be feared. He sold the Brook and went to New York City. That same year he was shot while playing cards in the Park Central Hotel and his records revealed that he was the financier and backer of gangsters involved in gambling, bootleg liquor, industrial rackets and narcotics.

72-73, Photographer unknown, 1900

Chefs from the Grand Union Hotel congregated at J. F. Hasenfuss Cafe on the corner of Congress and Federal Street. Notice the special street lamp and the man looking out of the second story window.

Joseph Hasenfuss was a bartender on Phila Street before he opened this Cafe and the Hotel Maine, which was at the same address. The 1899 City Directory states that it was "One block only from the Grand Union, Congress Hall, Congress Spring Park and Convention Hall. Recently refitted. Open year round." It was only listed in the Directory for five years. In the late 1930s it was known as the Moon Glow and later, until the 1970s, was Jimmy's Bar and Grill.

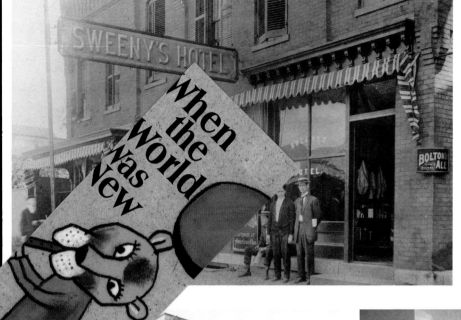

79-75, Photographer unknown, circa 1900

Sweeny's Hotel was located at 18-22 Railroad Place just across from the D.&H. Railroad Depot (the site was approximately between the Norstar Bank drive-in window and the Knights of Columbus Building). In later years the hotel was known as Hotel Millett.

The Sweenys were an outstanding hotel family from Saratoga Springs. John Sweeny ran Sweeny's Hotel. Later Edward C. Sweeny and his brother Martin continued the tradition. They were associated with the Berkshire, Chatam and Commodore in New York City, The Whitehall in Palm Beach, and the Worden, the Grand Union and the Gideon Putnam in Saratoga Springs. Martin was president of the Hotel Association of New York City.

9372/1, George S. Bolster, Photographer, 1939

The Worden Hotel stood at the northwest corner of Division and Broadway. In 1865 it was called the Marvin House and was described in a guide book as one of the best constructed hotels in Saratoga. It could accommodate three hundred guests. With a change of owners it became the Arlington. William W. Worden took over in 1885 and once again the name was changed and the hotel upgraded. In 1918 Edward C. Sweeny assumed the lease and in 1921 purchased the hotel. Under his management the rooms were equipped with plumbing, a telephone system was installed and a modern lobby and office were created. George Bolster worked at this very popular hotel and would frequently say that he received a free and very liberal education there.

59-445/4, George S. Bolster, Photographer, 1959

On December 1, 1959, the upstairs dining room of the Worden Hotel was the scene of a community tribute to writer and humorist Francis (Frank) Sullivan. It was arranged by Jean Clements of the library Board of Trustees and librarian Margaret Glasby. Representatives of Sullivan's illustrious class of 1910 from Saratoga High School attended. Messages came in from writers and friends throughout the country including Charles Brackett, Hollywood producer; James Thurber, writer; Thorton Wilder, novelist; John Kieran, writer and Mary Martin, actress.

In this photograph Mayor James E. Benton is leaning over talking to Sullivan. From left to right are Dr. Malcolm Magovern, master of ceremonies; Russell Crouse, a dramatist and close friend of Sullivan; Benton; Sullivan; John O'Hara, a novelist and Patricia Rose, who represented publisher Bennett Cerf. Sullivan's book called the "Moose in the Hoose" had just been published. It was originally intended for the Crouse children.

A genuinely witty but shy man, who did not like to make speeches, gave "a little gem of a talk," according to Anne Magovern. He started out saying "There are seven doctors and an undertaker here so it's all right to begin."

69

FRANK SULLIVAN
135 LINCOLN AVENUE
SARATOGA SPRINGS, N. Y.

Thursday

Dear Malcom,

After you left the other afternoon I
looked into the enclosed Recorder and lo, see who
was the Business Manager in 1915! Here it is, and
it may bring back some of your high school memories.

You said you wanted the names of some of the books
I have had published. I'll just mention the more
recent ones - my first book was published in 1925x 1925.
The latest of course is The A Moose In The House,
and before that, several years ago, "The Night The
Old Nostalgia Burned Down" ; and "A Rock In Every
Snowball", "A Pearl In Every Oyster" , one
called "Sullivan At Bay" which was published in
England; and one called "Sullivan Bites News."

Here's the biographical data, if you need it - Born
in Saratoga September 22, 1892 (on White Street).
Graduated high school 1910, from Cornell by the skin of
my teeth in 1914. Worked on The Saratogian from
1910, off and on, until army service in 1917 and
on leaving the army, went to New York in January
1919 and worked, successively, on the Herald, the
Evening Sun, and the World. When the World was sold
in February 1931, went to the New Yorker and
have worked for them and freelanced on the side
since then. *Came back to the old home town about 1935.*

I contributed to the New Yorker while I was still
on the World; in fact, I have contributed to the
Nyorkr since Harold Ross founded it in 1925 and am
therefore one of the original settlers as far as
that magazine is concerned. I believe there are
only three or four of us left who were contributors
to the magazine from its beginning.

This is probably all you need and more. I'm
delighted you are going to be the Boss Man. I'll feel
safe in your hands. You'll do a good job too. I
remember what a good job you did at the dedication
of the new high school at St. Peter's several years
ago. Love to Ann and the family.

Yours,

Frank

11889, *Michael L. Noonan, Photographer, copy of letter of November 1959*
   Anne Magovern had this letter in her files. It was written to Malcolm Magovern from Frank Sullivan before the community dinner honoring Sullivan. Dr. Magovern was master-of-ceremonies.
   Malcolm Magovern was a prominent physician in Saratoga Springs for many years. He had grown up in the city where his father, Thomas F. Magovern, was a photographer.

9372/3, George S. Bolster, Photographer, 1939
  The downstairs bar at the Worden was a legendary meeting place for both visitors and locals. Edward Sweeny hired Edward Buyck to paint some murals. In the grill area he had Buyck paint the area of the Worden as it looked in the 1800s, incorporating some of the buildings that were shown in Sweeny's collection of Kollner prints. On the west wall the painting was of the 1920 Traver's Stakes showing Man-Of-War beating Upset. He was tired of pictures showing "Big Red's" only defeat. Man-Of-War lost to Upset on August 13, 1919, but beat him four other times at Saratoga. The men sitting in front of the mural are not identified.

9372/4, George S. Bolster, Photographer, 1939
  This is a photograph of the downstairs bar at the Worden. Behind the bar on the top shelf are statues created by Bob Davidson, who was a regular patron and friend of Edward Sweeny. Bob Davidson taught sculpture at Skidmore College for many years.

4791/2, H. B. Settle, Photographer, 1922

Automobiles were the principal mode of travel to Saratoga Springs in the 1920s. Nearly fifty thousand patrons came to the racetrack and various gambling establishments. Single rooms in the Grand Union Hotel rented for fifteen to fifty dollars per day American Plan and cottage suites were a hundred dollars and up.

At the end of World War I, despite Prohibition, the climate for gambling hit its peak and casinos and speakeasys opened in Saratoga Springs and in former lake houses at Saratoga Lake. They offered low-priced meals, top-line entertainment and gambling. Limousine service was offered by all the hotels to these various establishments.

More Than a Resort

"AN UNNECESSARY OFFENSE"

In 1865, a Russian Jew named Benjamin Goldsmith made his way to Saratoga Springs. With a pack on his back and little else, Goldsmith started out in America as a peddler of "notions" — pins, needles and other items women needed at a time when nearly all sewing and mending was done at home. Twenty years later, Goldsmith was one of the most successful and respected businessmen in Saratoga; his store at 372 Broadway stocked the finest wines, liquors and cigars available, and he supplied many of the best hotels with the same. His was a success story that had happened before in America and would repeat itself countless times in the coming decades. And it was evidence of what a writer for Town and Country magazine had to say about people's perception of Saratoga, that it was inhabited just one month a year by the wealthy, who left behind a town that supposedly held its collective breath for the next eleven months: "Saratoga was by no means the exclusive preserve of the wellborn," Rena Niles wrote in 1954. "It is doubtful that it ever was — except in the imagination of its devotees."

Yes, life did go on in Saratoga Springs after the horses stopped running. People went on with their lives, doing what they had been doing before August and its attendant distractions became all-consuming. Saratoga, for all its lore of wealth and extravagance, has always been as ethnic a town as any in America.

Native Americans, English, Dutch, Scots, French Canadians, blacks, Germans, Irish, Jews, Italians, Poles — all have made Saratoga home over the past two centuries.

It was the Indians, the Iroquois in particular, who introduced the English, namely Sir William Johnson, to the springs that were to make Saratoga famous. Widely held to be the first white man to visit Saratoga, Johnson was certainly not to be the last. By the time the nineteenth century drew to a close, parts of all the great waves of immigrants flooding America eventually found their way to Saratoga.

Each new group faced the hardships and prejudices of their predecessors. Blacks had to take jobs as servants and waiters in Saratoga's many hotels because skilled jobs were denied them well into the twentieth century. The Irish, and after them the Italians, found work on the railroads and in other industries which were often the only jobs offered to the unskilled and uneducated immigrants. They lived in tight-knit neighborhoods concentrated on Saratoga's West Side, close to the big hotels and railroad lines. The black families for the most part established themselves along Congress Street and the Irish clustered nearby in a neighborhood that was home to so many Irish families that it became known as Dublin. By the 1920s, as the Italians moved in and the Irish left for other neighborhoods, Dublin became known as Little Italy. Each ethnic group formed their own social clubs and built their own churches and synagogues. They took care of their own and acted as their own boosters. An Irishman visiting America in the 1860s wrote of meeting some transplanted countrymen in Saratoga Springs and chronicled their successes in the New World so all on the Emerald Isle could bask in their accomplishments. That same writer, finally convinced by his friends to call on Chancellor Walworth, one of Saratoga's most esteemed citizens of the nineteenth century, handed Walworth a volume on Irish history and elicited this response: "Ah, my friend, your countrymen have suffered."

Despite Walworth's apparent love of the Irish, the visiting writer, Jeremiah O'Donovan, couldn't help himself and let slip a few sectarian jibes. Believing Walworth to be a Catholic because the chancellor's wife and children were practicing Catholics, O'Donovan found out otherwise, saying Walworth "sticks as fast and as tight to Protestanism as Prometheus did to the mountain." Despite their religious differences, O'Donovan thought highly of Walworth, and held out the hope that he too would convert to Catholicism, writing that "may God through his infinite goodness and mercy convert him from the errors of his ways. . ."

Tolerance of different races, ethnic groups and religions may have come easier for a place like Saratoga, a town known for going to just about any lengths to tolerate just about anything, as Sullivan observed in 1950: "Saratoga has seen so much of so many kinds of people that its attitude is less rigid and more tolerant than that of most small towns."

But it was an incident of intolerance that put Saratoga's name in newspapers across the nation for something other than horses and gambling. The controversy began with the opening of the 1877 summer season, when Wall Street financier Joseph Seligman brought his family to the Spa and tried to get accommodations at the Grand Union Hotel, where they had spent the past several summers. The hotel clerk informed the Seligmans that Judge Henry Hilton, executor of the estate of Alexander Stewart, recently deceased owner of the hotel, "has given instructions that no Israelites shall be permitted in the future to stop at this hotel." The judge's reasoning: allowing Jewish guests drove away Christian guests.

Banning Jews, and especially Joseph Seligman, who had helped finance the Union during the Civil War and bailed out the country during financial crashes in the 1870s, caused a furor. Anti-Semitism in America reared its ugly head in public for the first time. Reaction to Hilton's banning of Jews was met with editorials and outrage, though not all were in disagreement with Hilton. In fact, historian Lee M. Friedman said the Seligman incident provided "the starting point to articulate public expression of American anti-Semitism." It also gave an opportunity to oppose anti-Semitism, opposition that was reflected in the writings of such prominent authors of the time as Mark Twain and Bret Harte. Some of Seligman's peers in the banking world came to his defense after Hilton insinuated in a letter to the *New*

York Times that Seligman held little respect for those same peers. And Henry Ward Beecher, the brother of Harriet Beecher Stowe and the most prominent preacher of the time, railed against the insult made to a man the minister knew as a friend: "When I heard of the unnecessary offense that has been cast upon Mr. Seligman," Stowe said in a sermon, "I felt that no other person could have been singled out that would have brought home to me the injustice more sensibly than he."

The controversy was reportedly treated lightly by Seligman. Hilton was unrepentant. "I don't like this class . . . and don't care whether they like me or not . . . I believe we lose much more than we gain by their custom."

It was an ugly controversy that exposed an ugly truth: anti-Semitism existed in America and now it was out in the open. Some hotels in the Adirondacks followed Hilton's lead and declared their establishments closed to Jews. Four years after the furor, Seneca Ray Stoddard praised the Grand Union for its splendor yet mentioned its policy toward Jews in an almost off-handed manner: "This is a splendid example of the great American hotel, but it differs from most of them in the fact that it does not receive Jews as guests."

It is not known how the Seligman incident was viewed by the blacks who made up a majority of the hotel staffs in Saratoga; if anyone bothered to ask them, it was not saved for history's sake. Blacks were allowed in the hotels only to work as servants, bellhops, waiters and cooks. Accommodations were for whites only. By 1869, when Saratoga Springs could boast of thirty-three hotels and twenty-two boardinghouses in a village with a population of about seventy-five hundred, there were roughly three hundred blacks in the community. In the 1860 census, 76 percent of all black men worked in service jobs. Of the black women who worked, 96 percent held jobs as cooks, maids or in other capacities as domestics for white families.

In many of the hotels, most of the head waiters and bellmen were black. Many of the waiters were students at black colleges in the South, working during the summer to earn enough money to pay their way through school. One such student, with all the qualifi-

cations to teach school, could not get a job within the Saratoga school system in the late 1920s. As tolerant as its reputation may have been, Saratoga wasn't yet ready for such a thing.

Like other minority groups, Saratoga's black population formed its own clubs, established its own churches and had a neighborhood with a flavor all of its own. The Dunbar Social Club's membership boasted of the most educated blacks in the Spa. The establishment in 1863 of the African Methodist Episcopal Zion Church meant blacks could worship without being segregated into one corner, as was the practice when they attended services at white churches. And Congress Street, with its proximity to the downtown hotels, "was up all night long." Places such as the Tally Ho, Jimmy's Bar and Grill, the Carolina Club, the Hollywood and Jack's Harlem Club attracted both blacks and whites, including Skidmore College girls, who were forbidden to step foot on Congress Street but who flocked there nevertheless. Strippers, snake dancers, jazz bands, dancing girls, gambling, brothels — all were part of the action on Congress Street from the 1920s into the early 1950s. "There were more bars for such a short stretch of land than there was anywhere," recalled one man who worked as a waiter and bartender during Congress Street's heyday. "You could go all night from bar to club."

But with the 1960s came urban renewal, and with that came the end of Congress Street as the center of black life in Saratoga Spring. The old joints were bulldozed one after another. One landmark, Hattie's Chicken Shack, found a new home on Phila Street after nearly thirty years at the corner of Congress and Federal streets. An era that had begun more than a hundred years before, when the first freed slaves came to Saratoga to work the hotels, ended just a few years after those same hotels graced the Spa no more.

3511/D, H. B. Settle, Photographer, 1916

John McCormack was an Irish tenor who appeared in many productions of musical plays produced by Chauncey Olcott in the theater in Town Hall. In this photograph McCormack posed with Mrs. Olcott on the right and an unidentified woman on his left, possibly Mrs. McCormack. In the background was a cottage that was on the grounds of the Olcott estate "Inniscara" on upper Clinton Street. The cottage was reputed to have come from Ireland.

6013 detail, H. B. Settle, Photographer, 1928

T. W. Grippin Groceries was located at the corner of Caroline and Henry Street. The Daily Saratogian of October 1, 1889, stated that the United States Hotel purchased nineteen thousand dozen eggs at Grippin Groceries from June 18 to September 30. The largest number used in a single day was seven hundred dozen.

2977, H. B. Settle, Photographer, 1915
   Members of the prosperous Grippin family posed in front of their home at 157 Caroline Street (on the north side of the street between Marion and Nelson). The Grippins owned and operated businesses, principally Grippin Groceries and Saratoga Ice, which was an ice harvesting operation at Saratoga Lake.

82-96, W. H. Baker, Photographer, 1886

In 1982 an elderly woman named Deborah B. Chastain, came into the George S. Bolster studio with this photograph. She asked if this house still existed and where it was located. George assured her it did exist and showed her the location with photographs in his collection. She explained that her mother was the baby on the nurse's lap on the porch. Her mother's family had moved and had helped to settle Saratoga, Wyoming. She allowed him to copy the original photograph and George gave her a few of his "Old Saratoga" photographs,

including one of the Saratoga Vichy delivery wagon, to show Saratogians in Wyoming where they came from.

The Cluett House was at the corner of Clement and State streets. Although somewhat changed today, the house has been restored and remains a private residence. Families from Troy, New York, spent the season at their "summer cottages" which were clustered around the Clement, State Street, North Broadway area (where the North Side recreation field and Skidmore College playing fields are today).

62-277/8, Albert B. Hilton, Photographer, circa 1885

The Henry Hilton estate was located on North Broadway where the new Skidmore campus is today. Before Hilton, it was owned by Judge Henry Walton, who built a house above a pond called Denton's Vly (a Dutch word meaning marsh). He called the area Woodlawn. Later Henry Hilton built this mansion and thirteen other family mansions on Woodlawn, which is listed in the 1884 Saratoga Directory as a private park which ". . . contains about 300 acres laid out in walks, drives, ponds etc. by Hilton whose private residence is therein, and he allows the public access with private carriages."

The Vly was a boating and swimming pond. In the winter it was used by ice skaters and ice-boaters. Apparently Judge Hilton even supplied lanterns to illuminate the pond for a nighttime winter carnival.

The residence was luxurious with tapestries and bed coverings with "H" woven into them. In front of the house was a statue of Hiawatha done by noted American sculptor Saint-Gaudens. Hilton died in 1899 and the property eventually fell into disrepair. The pond was filled in and the mansion was destroyed by fire in 1959.

62-277/4, Albert B. Hilton, Photographer, 1885

An oriental carpet was laid out on the grass in front of Woodlawn, the Henry Hilton estate, for a formal portrait of the Judge and his family. Judge Hilton kept a flock of sheep complete with a Scottish shepherd in kilts and a collie on the property. In his boathouse on the Vly he had a variety of model boats. Over the years the Woodlawn Oval (the area where Wesley Health Care Center is today) was used for a variety of activities by the Saratoga Athletic Club.

75-128/4, Photographer unknown, 1887

George Sherman Batcheller was born in the Town of Edinburgh, Saratoga County in 1837. After graduating from Harvard, he came to Saratoga Springs to study law. In 1861 he married Catherine Cook of Albany, daughter of the state comptroller. During the Civil War he helped organize the 115th Infantry and became a lieutenant colonel. In 1873 he was elected to the New York State Assembly and in the same year built his famous house on Circular Street in Saratoga Springs. By 1875 he had become a judge and the American representative to the Court of First Instance of Cairo Egypt. For ten years his family lived in Egypt, then Washington and Portugal, where he was an ambassador.

75-46, Baker and Record, Photographers, 1873

The Batcheller mansion, at Circular Street and Whitney Place, was the first private home in the United States to be patented. The architects were Nichols and Hacott of Albany, New York. This photograph was taken while the house was being built. Notice the workmen standing on various joists. No expense was spared on the details of this home which had eleven bedrooms and five bathrooms.

73-61/3, Photographer unknown, 1874

Although the house was built before the Batcheller family lived in Egypt, an interest in the Middle East is evidenced in the cupolas, turrets and patterns on the house as well as the Arabic name given the house by Batcheller "Kasr-el-Nouzha," or "House of Pleasure." George, Catherine and eventually their only surviving child, Kate, entertained lavishly. Shortly after the house was built, U. S. Grant, president of the United States, was a guest.

2139, H. B. Settle, Photographer, 1913
The Walbridge family posed for a group photograph in front of 106 Lake Avenue, the home of Benjamin K. Walbridge, who was a lawyer. John H. was a real estate broker and John K. was the president and treasurer of the Saratogian and Saratoga County treasurer. They were all dressed elegantly for this family portrait; the men in hats, coats and gloves and the women in hats and furs.

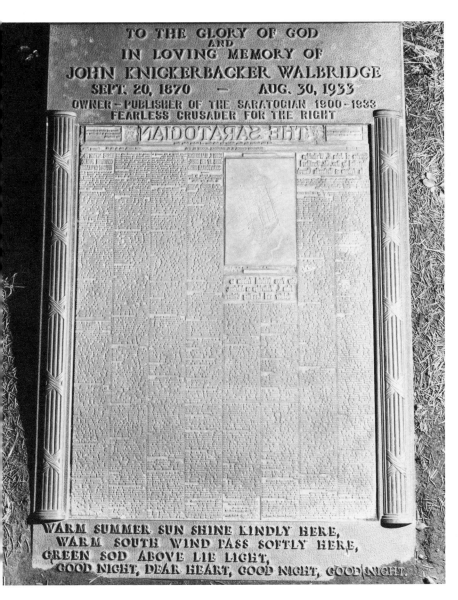

68-78, George S. Bolster, Photographer, 1968
This memorial marker in Greenridge Cemetery was dedicated to John Knickerbacker Walbridge (1870-1933). There was a front page obituary in the Saratogian on the date of his death. The printing plate was used as the marker so it appears backwards.

71-68, Photographer unknown, circa 1874
Above Terwilliger and Son Hardware (360 Broadway at the southeast corner of Broadway and Phila) was the Saratogian office. Later a skylight was put in this building and the space became home to a long line of photographers. By 1880 the Saratogian had moved to the Arcade Building where it advertised in the Saratoga Directory as "the only daily newspaper in Northeastern New York, the Daily Saratogian, sold for $7.00 a year by carrier with an average circulation of 1500 copies." The weekly Saratogian was published on Thursdays and cost $1.50 a year in advance. At the turn of the century the Saratogian moved to the current address at the corner of Maple and Lake Avenue.

5929, Harry B. Settle, Photographer, 1928

Originally the home of Dr. Charles S. Grant who died in 1899, the building was home to his widow Eliza and their daughter Amelia until 1904. Located at the northwest corner of Woodlawn and Walton streets, it was acquired by the Benevolent and Protective Order of Elks No. 161 as their home and clubhouse.

7351/2, H. B. Settle, Photographer, 1933

The Elks Club Magazine Good Will Tour from New York City to Milwaukee stopped in Saratoga Springs and was photographed in front of the Elks home on Woodlawn Avenue. The tour was sponsored by Studebaker and Firestone tires. A small banner above the running board advertises the upcoming "Elks National Convention, July 17."

By this time the front porches and the porte cochere had been removed from the house. Later all the porches were removed, and an addition was built on the north side of the building.

1309 detail, H. B. Settle, photographer, 1911
  Located on Lake Avenue, between Regent Street and Marion Place (where the Lake Avenue Elementary School is today) was the home of Lillian Ford Andrews. Her attic was reputed to be a stop on the "underground railroad," a route for blacks escaping from Southern slavery. In this recently discovered detail of the photograph of her attic, a fireplace complete with cooking utensils can be seen. On the right were a bed, candle and trunk, seeming to collaborate the story.

10.632/1, H. B. Settle, Photographer, 1944

The Daughters of the American Revolution was co-founded in Saratoga Springs by Ellen Hardin Walworth. They met at Pine Grove, the Walworth mansion, which was located at 523-527 Broadway. In this photograph, members are dressed in period costumes. The painting on the wall now hangs in the Historical Society of Saratoga Springs Museum with furnishings and artifacts from the Pine Grove estate, along with a detailed history of this interesting family.

The last chancellor of New York State, Reuben Hyde Walworth was head of the New York State Equity Court from 1828 to 1848. He held court in a wing of his Saratoga home. He and his wife, Maud, had five children. The youngest son, Mansfield, was a writer who married Ellen Hardin. After a tumultuous life, Mansfield abandoned his family. He was eventually murdered by his son (the Chancellor's grandson) who traveled from Pine Grove to New York City to do the deed.

Ellen Hardin Walworth opened a private school at Pine Grove in 1884. She became an expert on the Revolutionary War. By 1895 Pine Grove was advertised in the Saratoga Directory as "The Walworth," a boarding house with Corrinne B. Walworth as proprietor. By 1901 "The Walworth" listed George B. Ashton as proprietor. Ellen was still in residence. It stated: "The Walworth is one of the most attractive houses in Saratoga Springs. One hundred feet of front piazza and is convenient to all the principal springs, less than three squares north of the United States Hotel. It will be conducted in a first-class manner." The house was eventually torn down.

79/A, H. B. Settle, Photographer, 1904

The Gage-Ellis wedding was a glittering affair. In this photograph the wedding party was surrounded by plants and flowers and held horse shoes for good luck.

Augusta Gage was the daughter of Charles H. Gage, who was a partner in the firm of Gage and Hulin, manufacturers of the Hulin patent cooling and freezing refrigerator. They lived at Park Edge, North Broadway (now 779). She married William H. Ellis of Philadelphia.

5637, H. B. Settle, Photographer, 1926
    Hiram C. Todd was a lawyer who practiced in New York City. His family was socially prominent and owned a home at 4 Franklin Square in Saratoga Springs. Here the fashionably dressed family posed on a boat. Even after the Titanic disaster in 1912, Atlantic crossings and cruises remained popular.

6370, H. B. Settle, Photographer, 1929

This was the interior of the H. C. Todd House at the southwest corner of Franklin Square. One of the grand houses in Saratoga Springs, the living room was furnished with ornately carved rosewood furniture by John Henry Belter. Today these furnishings can be seen in a recreation of this room in the Historical Society of Saratoga Springs Museum in Canfield Casino in Congress Park.

2576, H. B. Settle, Photographer, 1914

After the formal portraits had been taken, the Schwarte family, in high good humor, had Harry Settle take some extra shots. This photograph was taken at 20 Fifth Avenue. Occupations of family members were listed as a teacher, lawyer, stenographer and a student at Cornell.

CHURCHES

78-21/12, Record and Epler, Photographers, 1884

    The governing body of the Presbyterian General Assembly met in Saratoga Springs in 1889. They assembled at the church which was listed in the 1884-85 Saratoga Directory *as "on Broadway, north of Town Hall. No pastor at present. Charles S. Lester, superintendent of Sunday School."*

    There are only two women in the picture. One is a young girl, holding her hat, on the left side of the photograph. Presumably she was attending with her father. The second is a black woman peeking out in the middle of the throng of men.

    The Presbyterian Church in Saratoga Springs was organized in 1817, with nine members, by the Presbytery of Albany.

9701, H. B. Settle, Photographer, 1941

The Presbyterian Church (later to become the Presbyterian New England Congregational Church) was located at 496 Broadway (where the parking lot between the Algonquin and Collamer buildings is today). It was first occupied by the Presbyterian congregation in 1857 and was used until it burned in 1976. The congregation purchased the Nolan House on Circular Street and constructed a modern church beside it.

Earlier Presbyterian churches were located at Woodlawn and Church Street and, in 1842, at the corner of Broadway and Caroline Street.

159, H. B. Settle, Photographer, 1905

The Methodist Church at 25 Washington Street was built in 1841 and originally had the tall spire shown in this photograph. In 1976 the United Methodist congregation built a new church at Henning Road and Fifth Avenue. This building is now used by the Universal Baptist Church. On the right is the building that is used as a parsonage by the Bethseda Episcopal Church which is located across the street.

73-185, Photographer unknown, circa 1920

The first Jewish Synagogue in Saratoga Springs was located in a building that had been the dining room of the Davardo, a boardinghouse located at the corner of Van Dam and Broadway. The **Saratoga Directory** listed the owner as Joseph Williams. According to Sophie Goldstein, who helped identify the photograph and who has been compiling a history of Jews in Saratoga Springs, the man's name was originally Willem. Most likely the name had been anglicized when he came to America.

The building was used as a synagogue from 1911 to 1926 when the temple and Jewish Community Center moved to Circular and Phila Street. On the right of the photograph is the home and office of Dr. George F. Comstock. The Comstock Building was taken down to make way for the Ramada Hotel and the City Center. The young woman in the photograph is not identified.

69-08, Photographer unknown, circa 1880

This building at 62 Henry Street has had a long history as a house of worship. Until 1901 it was the home of the New England Congregational Church. In 1901 St. Paul's German Evangelical Lutheran Church took over the building (the "German" was dropped in the early 1920s). By 1960 St. Paul's had moved to the new church on Lake Avenue. In the mid 1960s this church became the Soul Saving Station.

9365, H. B. Settle, Photographer, 1939
The Methodist Church choir was surrounded by greenery in this December 10, 1939, photograph taken at the church on Washington Street.

W92, J. S. Wooley, circa 1905
The First Baptist Church was erected in 1855. The 1880 Saratoga Springs Directory *described it: ". . . on Washington Street, opposite Federal Street, and near railroad crossing. Rev. George A. Smith, pastor. Services on the Sabbath at 10:30 and 7:30 p.m. Prayer meeting on Wednesday evening. Visitors always made welcome."*

In the large brick building in the left foreground, at 31 Federal, Mrs. Julia M. R. Young ran the Pleasant Home. Before becoming proprietor of this boardinghouse, she ran the Albermarle at 235 Broadway. Today a modern office building is on the site.

90

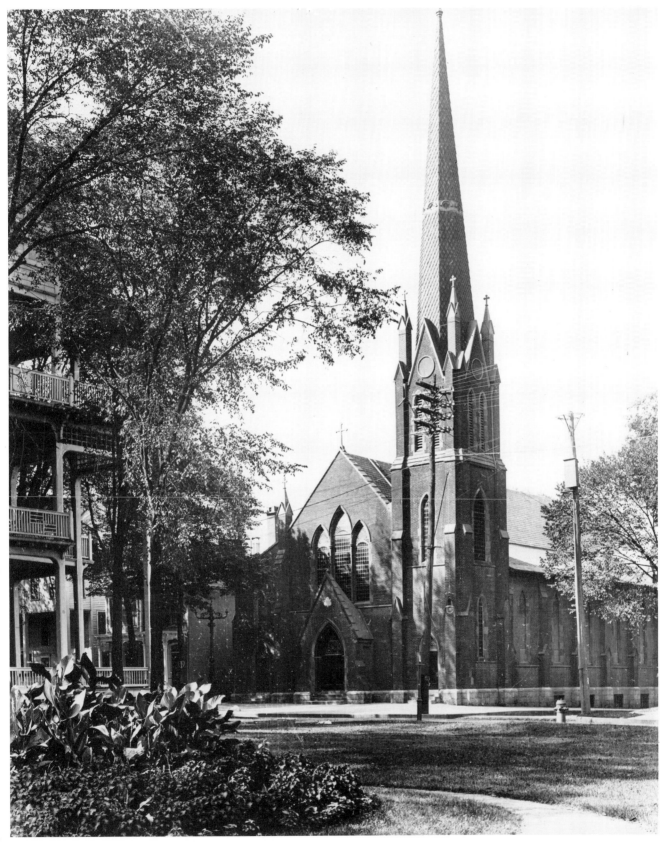

W21, J. S. Wooley, Photographer, circa 1905

The original spire of St. Peter's Roman Catholic Church, built in 1852, dominated the skyline in the South Broadway area. The spire was removed during a renovation in the early 1930s, a casualty of the high cost of upkeep and escalating fire insurance premiums. (Not a single spire remains in Saratoga Springs.)

A portion of a porch and garden that were part of the Windsor Hotel can be seen in the foreground.

11.247, H. B. Settle, Photographer, 1946

Students from Saint Peter's school sat for a pageant picture in 1946. A small portion of the interior of the church can be seen as it appeared after a 1930s renovation. In the early 1980s the interior was gutted and the church was remodeled to a "modern" design, in which the altar was moved into the center of the church.

52-18/1, H. B. Settle, Photographer, 1952

Bethesda Episcopal Church was incorporated in 1814. Rockwell Putnam gave the ground for the church which was generously supported by the Putnam family in its early years. J. Richard Upjohn was the architect of this Gothic Revival church. The first stone was laid in 1841. The nave was enlarged in the 1850s and in the 1880s the wrought-iron screen, shown in this photograph, was added to separate the congregation from the sanctuary.

The church is noted for its windows. Above the choir pews in the balcony are windows done by the Tiffany studios. The windows above the marble high altar were given by Spencer and Katrina Trask. They depict the healing miracle which took place at the pools of Bethesda, as described in the Gospel of John. Bethesda is an appropriate name for a church in Saratoga Springs which is famous for its healing springs and waters.

72-33, Photographer unknown, circa 1885
   Cemeteries were used as green spaces and parks, where families spent time strolling. The Greenridge Cemetery Chapel and Vault was built with Victorian ornamentation reflecting the architectural detail of buildings in the town. An 1880 plaque lists the Greenridge Cemetery Association: James M. Marvin, Pres., William B. Gage, Treasurer and George L. Ames, Superintendent.

65-182/1, Photographer unknown, circa 1905
This was the south side of Church Street looking east toward Broadway. There were a number of businesses on the street including W. A. Wilhelm, grocery and meats and Emery Fine Shoes. This area is now occupied by the Adirondack Trust Company. Across the street, in the area that is now the Post Office, was the Model Lunch Room, Manglesdorf Harness Shop and McNeary's Livery Stables. The Town Hall (now City Hall) had a clock and belltower which were removed in the mid 1930s.

70-130, Photographer unknown, circa 1890
Coley's Oyster House was located at 23 Phila Street. The Putnam Spring and Mineral Bath was next door. Notice the sign in front of the Oyster House. It was illuminated by gas, had holes in the end to admit air and a chimney on top as a vent.

4355, H. B. Settle, Photographer, 1920
    Over the years there were several oyster houses in Saratoga Springs. During the season fresh seafood arrived daily. Frank A. Hall was the proprietor of this lunch room and oyster house which was located behind the Worden Hotel and the United States Hotel livery and garage on Division Street at Woodlawn.

72-48, Photographer unknown, circa 1890
    The Printery, J. H. Reagan and Son, was located at 16 Caroline Street. Smith and Hickey Plumbing occupied the lower floor and Saratoga Dairy had a retail store next door.

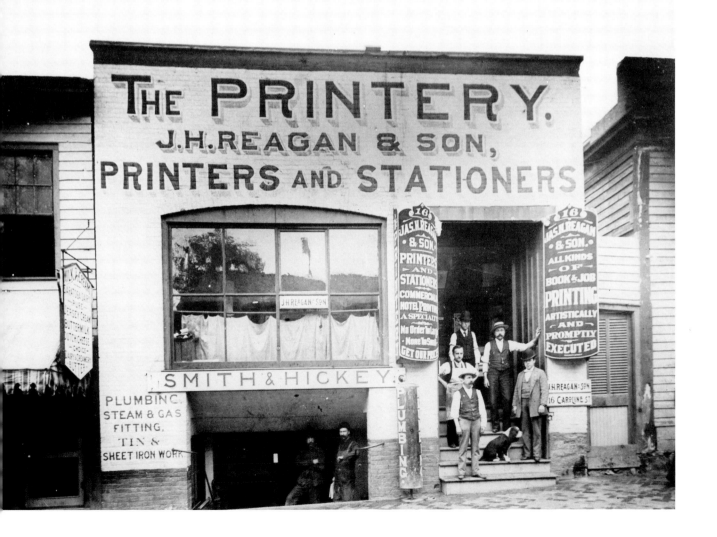

5734, H. B. Settle, Photographer, 1926

In this photograph, printed from a badly deteriorated negative, H. J. White Development Incorporated offered lots for sale in "the boom section of Saratoga." A sign says: "Have you seen the GEYSERS? Do you know why we have spent a fortune in buying property adjacent to the GEYSERS?"

What the company was speculating on was the development of Geyser Park by the state of New York. In 1916 the Conservation Commission was given the jurisdiction of the State Reservation at Saratoga Springs. The future of the Spa as a health resort looked bright and land speculation was inevitable.

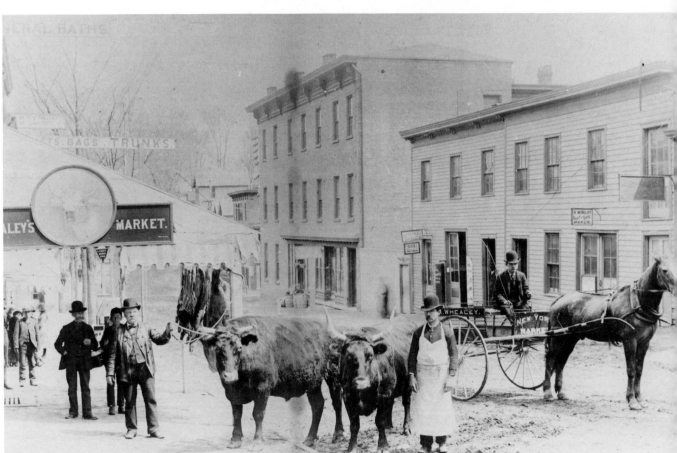

74-22/1, Photographer unknown, circa 1885

Whealey's Market was located at 21 Phila Street. Before 1883 it was located across the street at 14-16 Phila. The cattle in the photograph were soon to join the other carcasses hanging in front of the market. The delivery cart in front was ready to speed the fresh meat to homes or hotels. Across the street were R. Mingay Boot and Shoe Maker and Scoville Tailor Shop.

By 1899 Whealey had moved to 27 Caroline Street and in 1904 the Saratoga Directory lists the market at 4 Maple Avenue. There is no listing after 1906.

D71-48/2 detail, Photographer unknown, circa 1915
    This was the east side of Broadway looking south from Lake Avenue. On the corner, Menges and Curtis was already advertising itself as "The Old Store." In the front foreground was an old-fashioned streetlight and the cars were parked at an angle.

151A, H. B. Settle, Photographer, 1905

The Collamer Building on Broadway is today one of Saratoga Springs' outstanding restored commercial properties. In this 1905 photograph, it had balconies on the second floor which are not on the building today. From left to right, were: Farmer's Hardware; J. H. Mabbett and Company which sold dry goods; A. Wilhelm, groceries and meats; J. A. Beyer's Crockery Hall and Beyer's T. Store. In another photograph of the Beyer's T. Store window there were signs stating "Beyer the Beyer, Beyer the Seller, Beyer the Booster, Beyer the Peanut and Coffee Roaster" and "The People Come From Far and Near to Buy Fresh Roasted Peanuts Here." In 1940 Beyer's boasted that they had sold 9,660 pounds of peanuts.

J. A. BEYER'S
CROCKERY HALL.

BEYER'S T STORE.

BEYER'S
T
STORE.

Coffee Roasted Fresh Daily.

482 & 484 BROADWAY SARATOGA.

N° 7

70-136/5, Photographer unknown, 1923

Cars and carriages jammed Broadway around this "silent cop," the forerunner of modern traffic lights. Various businesses were located in the Shackelford Building on the east side of Broadway south of Phila Street: Well's Drug Store, United Cigars, Ensign's Dollar Store (crockery and household supplies), Marode's Candy Shop and the Clement's Hat Shop. In the corner building were Van Voast and Leonard, Dr. Leo Roohan, Sr., dentist and Gustave Lorey, photographer.

6083 detail, H. B. Settle, Photographer, 1928

On the northeast corner of Broadway and Caroline Street was McGirr and Company, millinery, which was in business until the 1980s. Next to it on the north side of Caroline Street was E. Holland, stationary and gifts, which is still in business. Following Holland's were the Lewis Meat Market, a bakery and the New York Bargain Store. On the south side of the street, Savard Brothers, Incorporated, sold men's clothing and furnishings and Rossi had a barber shop at 8 Caroline Street.

55-353/1, *Photographer unknown, 1940*

Haircuts, shaves, massages and manicures were all done in a busy day at the United States Hotel Barber Shop.

Franko (later Frank) T. Silvo opened a barber shop in the Worden Hotel at 417 Broadway in 1903. By 1909 he had relocated to the Arcade Building. After several different addresses on Broadway he returned to the Division Street side of the Worden by 1922. During the summer season he also operated the United States Hotel Barber Shop across the street. In the late 1940s he moved his business to the Gideon Putnam Hotel, working there until he retired in 1960.

7336/2, *H. B. Settle, Photographer, 1933*

This was the interior of the Paramount, which was situated on the southeast corner of Woodlawn and Church Street where the Adirondack Trust Company parking lot is today. Owner Peter Issaris was in business at this site until the mid 1960s. "Paramount Pete" landed in New York City from Greece in 1919 and spent the first years in America working in restaurants. The first one he owned was the Paramount in Queens, New York. Shortly after he opened his Saratoga Springs branch, he closed the Queens establishment to move north.

The Paramount was popular with Saratogians who liked to sit on the narrow Woodlawn Avenue porch for drinks. It was famous for lobster. In 1933 the price of a 1 and 1/4 pound lobster was one dollar. An ordinary dinner was fifty cents. The Marine Room in the back had dancing.

Later Peter Issaris bought the Ostrander mansion out Church Street and ran it as "The Dorian" until 1968. He sold the estate to the Saratoga Golf and Polo Club and it is now their clubhouse.

6539, *H. B. Settle, Photographer, 1930*

The 1935 Saratoga Springs Directory had an advertisement for the Happy Thomas Lunch Room at 458 Broadway: "Counter Service. Try Our 40 cent plate dinner. No expense has been spared in making this restaurant modern in every detail. Regular meals and a-la-carte in the heart of the business section."

101

6642/B, H. B. Settle, Photographer, 1930

This photograph shows the west side of Broadway south of Congress Street. In the background on the far right was the Grand Union Hotel, then the trolley station (the UCP Visitor's Center today) and the Columbian Hotel. In 1965 a fire started in the hotel, jumped the street and destroyed both the hotel and the Convention Hall.

The building that held Simon's was not destroyed. Lottie T. Zlotnick, owner of Simon's, married Max Katz who became the beloved proprietor of Katz's Newsroom. Known to generations of Saratoga school-children, "Mr. Katz" to the younger ones and "Max" to the high school students, he sold hot dogs and penny and nickel candy along with newspapers and magazines.

81-31/1 detail, Photographer unknown, 1888

Carriages filled the street in this 1888 photograph which captured many of the businesses on the east side of Broadway north of Division Street. Notice the gas lamps on the street. Behind the trees on the left was an election banner for Benjamin Harrison and his running mate, Levi Parsons Morton, who became the twenty-third president and vice-president of the United States. Harrison's term in office ran from 1889 to 1893. All the buildings in this photograph were destroyed by a fire in 1957.

7303, H. B. Settle, Photographer, 1933

On the east side of Broadway were the F. V. Hewitt and Sons grocery store and the F. W. Woolworth Company which was located in the E. D. Starbuck Building. This was the era when Woolworth only carried items which sold for five or ten cents. Starbuck's was a department store founded in 1886. At the turn of the century the upper floor of this building was home to the Masonic temple. From left to right, the first seven people are unidentified and beginning with the man in front of the Hewitt truck they are: Del Swart, Mark Shambo, George Kilcullen, unidentified delivery man for Swift Company, William Hoffman, Harris L. Mallery, Joseph Adams, Edgar F. Hewitt, Elizabeth Brown Traver, Thomas O'Dea, Mary McQuade, Madeline Ferguson Murray, unidentified Proctor and Gamble representative, unidentified, William Gyngell, William Toussant, _____ Cummings and three unidentified people.

5574, H. B. Settle, Photographer, 1926

E. D. Starbuck, Sr. (left), and E. D. Starbuck, Jr. (right), were surrounded by their employees in this photograph taken in the backyard of the Starbuck home at 11-Fifth Avenue. The Starbucks owned a popular department store at 408-412 Broadway.

57-306A/13, George S. Bolster, Photographer, 1957

Onlookers, in the foreground of this photograph, turned away in tears as buildings on the east side of Broadway were consumed by fire. The roof of the E. D. Starbuck building at 408-418 Broadway was lifted completely off the building by flames and hot gases before it crashed down. Patrolman Fred E. Pettit was killed and Fire Chief Robert Carroll was seriously injured. Five other firemen were also injured and a sixth suffered a heart attack. A total of seven buildings were consumed by the nighttime fire which started in a bowling alley at the rear of Palace Recreation at 398 Broadway.

57-306B/19, George S. Bolster, Photographer, 1957

The next day, residents of the city viewed the devastation caused by the fire.

59-298/7, Photographer unknown, circa 1905

A woman from the Salvation Army, holding a newspaper called War Cry, *stood on the northeast corner of Phila and Broadway. The Citizen's National Bank was behind her. It later became Saratoga National Bank. The United States Hotel was in the background.*

The Salvation Army has had a long history in Saratoga Springs. On October 16, 1889, nearly a thousand people gathered on the third floor of Town Hall to attend a reunification ceremony for the Salvation Army. At that time there had been two splits within the Salvation Army. The first occurred in 1884 over constitutional issues and a second occurred in one of the splinter groups. Saratoga Springs was chosen as the site for the reconciliation because of the reputation of the healing qualities of the waters. A centennial celebration was held in Saratoga Springs in 1989.

70-115, Gustave Lorey, Photographer, 1933

Officers and staff of the reorganized Saratoga National Bank posed for a formal photograph. Seated from left to right are: Andrew M. Douglas, cashier; Louis W. Noland, president, and William J. Brennan, assistant cashier. Standing, second row, are: Helen Schwartz, Andrew J. Isolda, Katherine F. McQuade, Dorothy K. Ericson, Alfred W. Stannard, Frederick J. Hamell, Helen A. Hayes, Marion C. Blodgett, James J. Lynch, Agnes R. Fish, Douglas H. Williams and Bertha M. Smith. In the rear are: Frederick J. Phillips and William J. Hickey.

10-369/1 Detail, H. B. Settle, Photographer, 1943

Nathan "Nate" Goldsmith, with his trademark cigar, is shown as he sat on a chair outside his luncheonette and delicatessen at 37 Phila Street. He was a well-known restaurateur who later moved his establishment to 43 Phila Street where it was known as Mother Goldsmith's or "Mother's" to generations of Saratogians. In later years he also built and owned the Country Gentleman on South Broadway. Nate retired from Mother's in 1988.

Produce was piled up on the sidewalk next door to Goldsmith's. This corner location was home to many grocery stores over the years. In 1943 it was Tanenbaum's store. Prior to that it was Warings and "Reliable" Grocery with George Serotta as proprietor.

2003, H. B. Settle, Photographer, 1913

The "Tarrant Group" was photographed outside the plant at Ash and Franklin streets (25-27 Ash Street). By 1924 Tarrant Manufacturing Company with William P. Tarrant, president, had moved to 27 Jumel Place. It advertised welding and road building supplies. William P. Tarrant also owned a plumbing and steam fitting shop at 12 Maple Avenue. Later Fredrick Tarrant became president and by the mid 1960s the company was operating at Jumel Place and at 4 Excelsior Springs Avenue. The business continues at the Excelsior Springs address today.

W132, J. S. Wooley, Photographer, circa 1915

The Clark Textile Works was located on High Rock Avenue between High Rock Spring and the Old Red Spring on the site of the Empire (or Emperor) Spring. It was later purchased by the Van Raalt Company and eventually became the Saratoga Knitting Mill. The trolley ran beside the building and went as far as Glens Falls.

The photographer, Jesse Sumner Wooley (1867-1943), was located in Ballston Spa. Before Harry Settle set up his own business in Saratoga Springs in 1900, he worked for Wooley. Wooley's son sold some of Wooley's five-by-seven glass-plate negatives and postcard-size nitrate negatives of Saratoga Springs to George S. Bolster. Many of his other photographs are in the Saratoga County Historical Society Museum at Brookside in Ballston Spa.

82-26/4, Photographer unknown, circa 1875

The Saratoga Waterworks was located on Excelsior Avenue at the corner of Marion Avenue. It was built in 1871 and had a tower that was similar in appearance to the ones on Town Hall and the D.&H. Railroad Station which were built at the same time. Today this building has become part of the Saratoga Dairy, owned by Stewart's Ice Cream Company, Inc.

51857/26, George S. Bolster, Photographer, 1957

In May 1957, John "Hawkeye" Hart, star of the film series Hawkeye, the Last of the Mohicans, *made a tour of the Stewart's stores in the tri-city-Saratoga area. Stewart's had sponsored the series on WRGB, T.V.*

In 1922 the Dake brothers, C. V. and P. W., operated a dairy farm near Daketown. They bought the equipment for the manufacture of ice cream from the old Thomas Ice Cream and Candy Company and combined it with their dairy business. During the first year they sold twenty-five hundred gallons of "Dake's Delicious Ice Cream." General Ice Cream Company of Schenectady bought the business and carried on under the Dake name until 1956.

In 1945 the original Dake brothers plus Charles S., who was a decorated veteran back from World War II, bought Don Stewart's business. Under the Stewart's name the company sold thirty-five

thousand gallons of ice cream the first year. In 1953 alone they opened twenty-two new stores and were operating a bottling plant, Saratoga Dairy, and a modern ice-cream plant.

On May 15, 1956, the ice cream plant suffered a quarter million dollar fire, but by October 21, ten thousand people attended an open house at the completely rebuilt and remodeled facility. In the late 1940s the Stewart's organization was expanding its stores to "The New Look" and introduced the "make your own sundae." The ice-cream cartons were red, white and blue with a drawing of the Saratoga ice-cream plant decorating the front of the packages.

The business remains in the Dake family. William P. Dake is president of a company that has over 170 stores in New York and Vermont and processes 250,000 gallons of milk per week for its various products.

69-114, George S. Bolster, Photographer, 1969

A few days before Urban Renewal destroyed the building, George Bolster went to Hattie's Restaurant on 7 South Federal Street and coaxed Hattie outside to be photographed in front of her renowned "Chicken Shack." Hattie Moseley Austin served dinners to all types of Saratogians and visitors throughout the years. She relocated to 48 Phila Street and is still in business.

South Federal Street ran from Congress to West Circular streets. The portion of the street where Hattie's was located no longer exists.

E D U C A T I O N

72-204/2, Photographer unknown, 1874

The 1874 graduating class of Saratoga High School had four women and two men and was taught on the first floor of School No. 4, at the corner of Spring and Court streets.

The following year, high school was taught at the "Old Gas House," just west of the present Lake Avenue firehouse. In 1884 a new high school opened on Lake Avenue. It was on the site of today's firehouse. In 1924 the high school moved up the street to a new building between Regent Street and Marion Place. Currently that building serves as the Lake Avenue Elementary School.

6627, H. B. Settle, Photographer, 1930

This class reunion photograph was commissioned for W. E. Benton on June 24, 1930. The reunion was described in the Saratogian. "With 31 of the 46 surviving members of the class who received diplomas of graduation in attendance, the Class of 1910 was entertained yesterday by William E. Benton, one of its members, in reunion. . . .

Accompanied by the wives and husbands, members of the class gathered during the late afternoon at the beautiful summer home of Mr. and Mrs. Benton, Farvue Lodge, on the Middle Grove Road,

west of the city, where the time until 9 o'clock was busily occupied in renewing acquaintances and enjoying the beauty of the estate."

The news article goes on to describe the estate, the planting of a class tree and a dinner at which Frank Sullivan was toastmaster. At 11 o'clock they went to the Congress Theater, owned by Mr. Benton, for a special showing of the talking picture So This is London featuring Will Rogers. This illustrious class included, besides Benton and Sullivan, Dr. John Heslin, Mary Robbins Richardson, Edgar Starbuck and Charles W. Brackett.

74-82, Gustave Lorey, Photographer, 1923
In 1923 there were sixty graduates of the Saratoga Springs High School. Many of them became prominent in Saratoga Springs life.

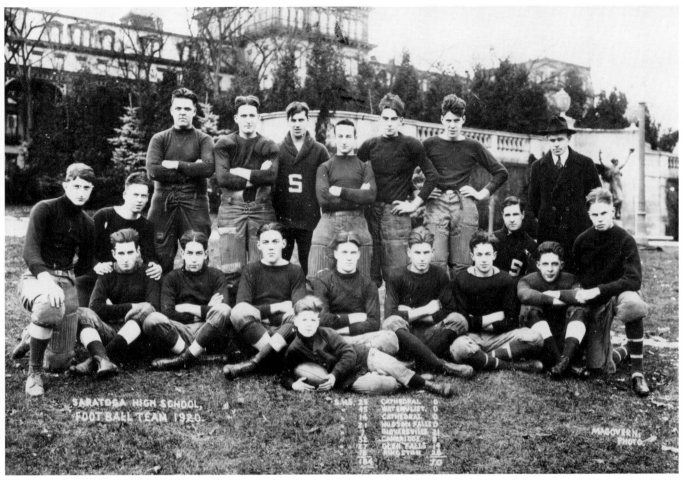

11.667, Thomas F. Magovern, Photographer, 1920

In this photograph, the High School football team posed in Congress Park. In the background, the Grand Union Hotel rose impressively and the Spirit of Life can be seen on the right.

9982, H. B. Settle, Photographer, 1942

Budding artists were hard at work in Mrs. Florence Hall's classroom in School No. 3.

72-204/1, Thomas F. Magovern, Photographer, 1924

    The Saratoga Springs public school system has had fine music programs for many years. In 1924 the grade school orchestra posed for a photograph. In the 1924 Saratoga Directory, Irene E. Winne was listed as the music teacher. Apparently the five elementary schools shared the special teachers in music, domestic science, drawing and penmanship, manual training and physical training.

51-165, H. B. Settle, Photographer, 1951
The Saratoga Springs Convention Hall was used for graduations until it burned in 1965. In front of the graduates, the senior choir presented its part of the program.

12.092, H. B. Settle, Photographer, 1948
This is a photograph of the St. Clement's School eighth grade graduating class of 1948.

In the 1870s and 1880s the Glen Mitchell Hotel was located out North Broadway near the Saratoga Agricultural Fairgrounds. In 1893 this hotel became the St. Clement's College and Mission House of the Redemptorist Fathers. In 1918 a listing appeared for St. Clement's Church on Lake Avenue: it included the parochial school, St. Clement's College Mission House and the church. By 1923 the North Broadway address was called St. Clement's Farm.

In 1952 the St. Clement's Infirmary and Rest Home was added (it is now the St. John Newmann Residence) and in 1965 the College was dropped from the name.

113

9415, H. B. Settle, Photographer, 1940

St. Peter's High School graduates posed for their graduation picture in 1940. It was the era of bobby socks and saddle shoes with only one non-conformist in the front row.

6255, H. B. Settle, Photographer, 1929

In 1929 the Saratoga Eastman School of Business opened in the National Bank Building at 366 Broadway with Harry M. Spamer as director. It was still listed at the same address in 1941 but offered a letter service, mimeographing, multigraphing, and stenotype supplies.

2773, H. B. Settle, Photographer, 1914

St. Faith's School was started by Beatrice Sands, Eleanor Shackelford, Dr. Carey (the minister of Bethesda Church), and a Sister Gertrude, with three little girls as students. It was built in a grove of oaks on property that had been willed by Gideon Putnam. Eleanor Shackelford was a descendant of the original Putnam family. Dr. Carey blessed the school on Ascension Day in 1891.

In the 1944 Saratoga Directory, Saint Faith's School was advertised at 17 Seward Street, with the Rev. Leonard W. Steele, principal, offering ". . . complete educational, social and religious training for girls. There are accommodations for about 50 boarders and a few day pupils are also taken. Work is offered from the third grade through high school. The emphasis is on thorough preparation in the basic subjects so that pupils will be ready for specialization in college or other higher institutions."

By 1947 there were only two graduates and the school was closed. Louis J. Farone bought the property and in 1965 Irving Metzger purchased six acres which became Franklin Garden apartments and professional offices in the Van Rensselaer Street area.

2029, H. B. Settle, Photographer, 1913
    Mrs. J. B. "Lucy" Scribner and Miss Smith were photographed in Lucy Scribner's home on North Broadway. The house was recently refurbished and currently serves as the home of the president of Skidmore College. Skidmore College has had only five presidents in its history: Charles Keyes, Henry Moore, Val Wilson, Joseph Palamountain and David Porter, the current president.

1095, H. B. Settle, Photographer, circa 1910

At the turn of the century, the textile industry could provide young women with gainful employment. Lucy Scribner, who had come to Saratoga to regain her health, recognized this and started the Young Women's Industrial Club to provide training in all phases of the industry to young women.

This photograph shows Mrs. Week's sewing group. Behind the women, who were learning handiwork, was a dressmaker's dummy and textile machines.

The first building purchased for the Young Women's Industrial Club was the former Temple Grove Seminary, a seminary for young women, at the corner of Circular and Spring streets. The seminary had been founded in 1856 with Rev. C. F. Dowd as principal. (Dr. Dowd was credited with originating and promoting the system of Standard Time which has been used in the United States from 1883 to the present). The building was renamed Skidmore Hall and today is an apartment building.

82-12, Hank Myers, Photographer, Middle Falls, N.Y., 1949

The scene of many plays and concerts, this building was the first one built expressly for the Young Women's Industrial Club in 1903. It had an auditorium and gymnasium on the upper floor, while the lower level held the textile machines used for instruction. There was an alley that ran down the middle of the building that was probably used for bowling.

When the building was converted to the Little Theater of Skidmore College, the props and flats for the stage were stored in the lower level and lifted up to the stage by a pulley system through a hole cut in the floor.

When Skidmore moved to the new campus, the building was closed and eventually fell into disrepair. It was then taken over by the Saratoga Springs Preservation Foundation who stabilized it and attempted to find a purchaser. It was finally acquired by Williard E. Grande and readapted for use as a Museum of Antiques and Art and, more recently, the Regent Street Antique Center.

2597/4, H. B. Settle, Photographer, 1914
Sporting middy outfits, the Skidmore School of Arts tennis team posed for a photograph.

2528, H. B. Settle, Photographer, 1913
Students at the Skidmore School of Arts were hard at work in a drawing class. Replicas of classical sculpture surrounded them and the display board in the background showed completed design exercises.

1572, H. B. Settle, Photographer, 1912

This was the 1912 graduating class of the Skidmore School of Arts. Before 1911 the college was called the Young Women's Industrial Club and in 1922 it became Skidmore College.

In this photograph, high-buttoned shoes peeked out under the hemlines of demure white dresses. These early photographs were taken in an eight-by-ten-inch format on glass-plate negatives. Over the years some of the glass plates were broken.

7479/9, H. B. Settle, Photographer, 1933

The 1933 graduating class of Skidmore College lined the sidewalk in front of the Skidmore Little Theater building on Regent Street to greet the faculty as they paraded to graduation exercises in College Hall. Dr. W. David Howe, chairman of the Board of Trustees, conferred the first honorary degree ever awarded by Skidmore College: a doctor of laws to Dr. Henry T. Moore, president of Skidmore. Dr. Howe stated, "During a period of more than a quarter of a century we have seen the development of our college, which in many ways has been notable. It is our conviction that during the next quarter century our college will develop in a manner of which we may all be equally proud . . . . we have unbounded confidence in our faculty and in our president. We have an ever increasing body of loyal alumnae." (Saratogian June 4, 1933)

55-10/6, George S. Bolster, Photographer, 1955

Dormitory life seemed cozy and comfortable in the old homes on Union Avenue that served as Skidmore dormitories. Housekeeping was immaculate if the shine on the coffee table is any indication.

In 1961 the college trustees and President Wilson decided to abandon the eighty-two charming but inefficient buildings in the heart of Saratoga Springs and build a new campus in the wooded hills in the northwest corner of the city. The funds for the purchase of the 650 acre tract, the former Henry Hilton estate, were donated by Margaret and J. Erik Jonsson, the parents of a Skidmore student. Construction began in November 1963 but Val Wilson died before the first building was completed. Josephine Case, president of the Board of Trustees, served as interim president for fifteen months. In July 1965, Dr. Joseph Palamountain arrived in Saratoga Springs to assume the leadership of Skidmore College. From that date until 1987 when he retired, the college underwent unprecedented change and growth: forty-seven buildings on the new campus, the doubling of the student body, near doubling of the faculty, tripling of the library collection, an increase in endowment and a change to co-education.

W112, J. S. Wooley, Photographer, 1910

A series of photographs was taken for postcards in 1910 by J. S. Wooley, a very fine photographer from Ballston Spa. This one is a view of the Yaddo fountain and mansion.

Spencer Trask and his wife, Katrina, bought five hundred acres of land in Saratoga Springs in 1881 and renovated an Italian villa-style wooden house on the property. Then tragedy struck. In 1889 Mrs. Trask contracted diphtheria at her home in Brooklyn. She survived but unfortunately allowed her four children to visit her in quarantine too soon. They contracted the disease and died. Shortly after, in 1891, Yaddo burned to the ground. Katrina became an invalid.

With indomitable spirit, the Trasks decided to rebuild Yaddo and had the fifty-five-room Victorian Gothic mansion, pictured in this photograph, constructed. The architect was William Halsey Wood who incorporated stained glass windows by the Louis Comfort Tiffany and Charles Lamb Studios in the building. The rose gardens, open to the public, were laid out in 1899.

In 1900 the Trasks made a decision to create the Corporation of Yaddo to preserve it as a permanent retreat for artists, writers and musicians.

The retreat opened in 1926 with Elizabeth Ames as its director. She remained at Yaddo for forty-five years.

Approximately fifteen buildings and studios now make up the complex which has provided free time and space for an extraordinary number of America's most important cultural figures.

73-145/52, Photographer unknown, circa 1900

Katrina and Spencer Trask were photographed sharing a quiet moment playing chess at Yaddo. Both Trasks were gifted people. Katrina wrote and published poetry, novels and plays. Spencer was a talented photographer. Visiting writers and artists attended the many Trask house parties and masques.

In a tribute to him, after his tragic death in 1909, the Saratoga Sun stated, "Mr. Trask was not simply a shrewd financier and able businessman. He was an idealist as well, being moved by profound impulses to make the world better and more beautiful...such would be the man to finance an Edison, as he did; a great newspaper; a book publishing house; to found a noble country estate; to love art and nature with passion; and, when retired from active business, to take up such work as developing Saratoga Springs as a great health resort."

At the time of his death, Spencer Trask was just beginning to recover financially from the depression of 1907. Katrina lived frugally for many years to preserve as much money as she could for Yaddo. In 1921 she married her husband's banking partner and her longtime friend and admirer, George Foster Peabody. She died the following January.

71388, Michael L. Noonan, Photographer, 1988

This is the Yadoo group picture of guests in the summer of 1988. Each year approximately 165 artists, writers and musicians become "fellows" at Yaddo. All are expected to concentrate on their work in a nurturing, supportive environment. Lunch is supplied in a thermos and tin pail. Dinner is served in the large Trask dining room in the summer when there are about thirty to forty guests. In the winter the mansion is closed and the ten to fifteen artists dine in the winter dining room.

4201/1, H. B. Settle, Photographer, 1919

Built in 1889 by Franklin W. Smith, the House of Pansa was a replica of the home of a wealthy nobleman buried in the ruins of Pompeia, Italy, when Mount Vesuvius erupted in 79 AD. Smith traveled to Europe many times, commissioning artists and historians to reproduce the architecture, statues and paintings that would show the life of a Roman nobleman.

When the House of Pansa opened on August 12, 1889, the New York Herald Tribune said "The building is a monument that will take its place with the most impressive and unique contributions to the art of this country." The Daily Saratogian said "This reproduction of a Roman house will certainly become famous throughout the world."

In the George S. Bolster Collection are other plans that Smith had developed for a grand park in Saratoga Springs. Before they could be realized, he went bankrupt and the House of Pansa closed its doors in a 1906 foreclosure.

In 1914 the building was purchased by the Masonic Hall Association and became the home of the Masons for thirty years. A fire on Christmas eve in 1926 destroyed many of the relics. One hallway featured Egyptian murals and artifacts. George Bolster was then a child and vividly recalled the police chasing the kids away from the Egyptian mummies that lay smoldering on the street.

The Masons sold the building to a group representing the Congregation Shaarei Tefilah in 1952. They remodeled it for use as a Synagogue and Jewish Community Center which they used until 1989. The future of the building is currently uncertain.

An interesting side note to this building occurred in the late 1960s when the Saratoga County YMCA was built next to the former House of Pansa. Franklin W. Smith, the original builder of the House of Pansa, was also the founder of the Young Men's Christian Association in America.

71-118/14, Photographer unknown, circa 1900

From earliest times Saratoga Springs was a city associated with health and healing. Naturally many private clinics and hospitals developed to care for the infirm who came for the waters and the fresh air that was considered beneficial to health. This building was the McCarty Hospital. Today it is the Washington Inn.

71-119/2, Photographer unknown, circa 1855
  The Stanwyx Hotel stood at the southwest corner of Broadway and Congress Street where the U.C.P. Visitor's Center is today. It later became Dr. Bedortha's Sanitorium, the "Water Cure." On July 4, 1854, a small boy tossed a firecracker through the window which caused an explosion and fire that raged for twelve hours destroying fourteen buildings in the area.

80-127, Photographer unknown, circa 1890
  St. Christina's Home and Hospital for crippled children was located on Ballston Avenue approximately where the K-Mart Shopping Plaza is today. It was supported by Spencer and Katrina Trask and was in operation from 1878 to 1925.

71-118/12, Photographer unknown, circa 1900
  After 1890 this building at 2 Franklin Square was listed as the home and office of Dr. Robert C. McEwen. At the time of this photograph it was called the Adirondack Lodge. Today it has been readapted for use by a variety of businesses and is a keystone building in the revitalization of Franklin Square.

11-330, H. B. Settle, Photographer, 1946

Before Saratoga Hospital moved to its current location on Church Street in 1913, it used this building which was at the corner of Division and West Harrison. In 1895, Mrs. C. S. Lester was president and A. C. Rich was treasurer with Mrs. H. B. Rich as secretary of the hospital. After the hospital moved, the building became a hotel under a variety of names. It fell into disrepair and was torn down in the 1970s.

59-145B, George S. Bolster, Photographer, 1959

When Saratoga Hospital moved to Church Street in 1913 it was located in the country. By 1959, when this aerial photograph was taken, it was still at the edge of the city. On the left is Cramer House, which was the home of the nursing school.

George S. Bolster did a fairly extensive group of aerial photographs of the city which dramatically show the growth that has occurred since the 1950s and early 1960s.

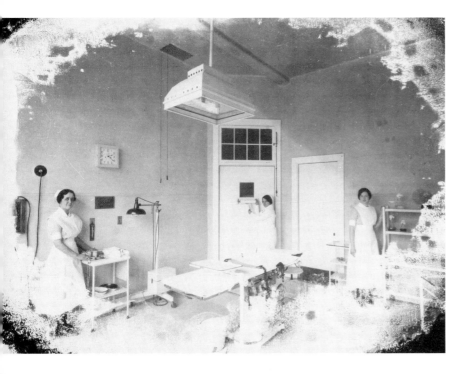

6272, H. B. Settle, Photographer, 1929
Nurses-in-training rotated through the various departments of Saratoga Hospital. Two of them are shown with their supervisor in the operating room in this photograph made from a deteriorated 1929 negative.

5757, H. B. Settle, Photographer, 1927
By today's standards, the 1927 Saratoga Hospital laboratory was a fairly simple place. Natural light was used by the lab technician on the left to illuminate her microscopic slides. Notice the rack of washed test tubes in front of the sink.

12-573, H. B. Settle, Photographer, 1949

One of the major industries in Saratoga Springs for seventy-eight years was the Harvey Manufacturing Company which manufactured more than fifteen hundred pharmaceutical products including Saratoga Ointment, tablets, pills, fluid medicines, lozenges, powders and suppositories.

George S. Harvey, a pharmacist and inventor, came to Saratoga Springs in 1875. From 1880 to 1885 he worked from his home at 162 Church Street using his barn as a laboratory. In 1889 he bought an old gristmill at Wells and Waterbury streets and in 1890 the G. F. Harvey Company was incorporated.

In "Saratoga Springs History" in the Saratogian of July 12, 1989, City Historian Martha Stonequist describes the Harvey Company process: "In this new plant pills were coated individually by hand in the gelatin coating room. Each pill was placed on a needle and dipped in gelatin. Sugar-coated pills were dipped in five kettles containing sugar in syrup form and another four kettles were used to polish the products. Hand machines rolled up to 10,000 tablets a day; by 1930, one machine could turn out 200,000 pills daily."

The Harvey Company was one of the first employers in Saratoga to offer group insurance and accidental health coverage to its employees. The company was liquidated in 1958. Saratoga Ointment is still made by Blair Laboratories of Norwalk, Connecticut. The building has been readapted and is used for professional offices.

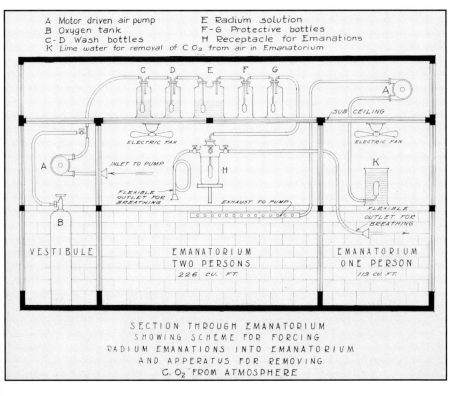

A Motor driven air pump E Radium solution
B Oxygen tank F-G Protective bottles
C-D Wash bottles H Receptacle for Emanations
K Lime water for removal of C O₂ from air in Emanatorium

SECTION THROUGH EMANATORIUM
SHOWING SCHEME FOR FORCING
RADIUM EMANATIONS INTO EMANATORIUM
AND APPERATUS FOR REMOVING
C. O₂ FROM ATMOSPHERE

3461/1, H. B. Settle, Photographer, 1916

Dr. Douglas Moriarta had an office at 511 Broadway and a private hospital at 113 Phila Street. This drawing of a "Radium Emanatorium" was in the George S. Bolster Collection. Whether it was ever built or used has not been determined.

Floyd "Whitey" McMillian, a forty-year employee of Saratoga Hospital, remembered that Dr. Moriarta was the first physician, that he knew, to use radium. In the early 1940s, Mr. McMillian was working in the nursing department of the hospital. Dr. Moriarta had placed a two-by-two-by-four-inch block on the abdomen of a cancer patient and asked Mr. McMillian to remove it at a certain time. Not knowing what it was, he removed it and placed it on the window sill behind a curtain. The next day he received a phone call at home asking what had become of the block of radium. Dr. Moriarta was concerned because it was worth twenty thousand dollars. Obviously the dangers of radium exposure were not yet known. According to Mr. McMillian, Dr. Moriarta died of old age and was not affected by his exposure to it.

58-353/5, George S. Bolster, Photographer, 1958
Clean air and sunshine awaited these "Fresh Air Kids" from big cities who arrived at the railroad station to be greeted by their Saratoga Springs sponsors.

129

Unnumbered, George S. Bolster, Photographer, circa 1950

The Hawley Home for Children was located at 64-66 Ludlow Street for sixty-one years. It was begun in 1888 by Augusta P. Wiggins who took care of a few children who were orphaned or not well cared for at home. It was first housed in the Home of the Good Shepherd and moved several times. By 1891 it was incorporated by the State Board of Charities and named the Saratoga Home for Children.

In "Saratoga Springs History" in the Saratogian of November 8, 1989, City Historian Martha Stonequist writes: "Hawley was elected president of both the trustees and managers. A house on Mitchell Street was purchased for $3,500, with room for 14 children, the matron and her helpers. Hawley described the object of the Home: 'to receive, to care for, and to educate indigent and orphan children that are between 18 months and 10 years of age. This includes such management and training as belong to a well-regulated family. The discipline is parental,'"

She goes on to state that the Mitchell Street location became overcrowded and that the building on Ludlow was purchased, opened in 1906 and renamed the Hawley Home for Children. It continued in operation until 1965 when it was unable to comply with state and county laws. An endowment of approximately five hundred thousand dollars is administered by the Hawley Foundation to assist individuals and organizations in Saratoga County that deal with children.

85-68/3, Michael Noonan, Photographer, 1985

The newest health care facility in Saratoga Springs is Four Winds-Saratoga, a private psychiatric hospital located off Route 9 south of Cresent Avenue. Dr. Xavior Mastrianni, executive and medical director, spoke at the ground breaking ceremony in 1985. Four Winds Hospital treats patients of all ages and has units specializing in the treatment of adolescents and college age students. There is a secondary school at the hospital and, in a unique program with Skidmore College, college-age students continue their studies while receiving treatment at the hospital. The owners of Four Winds Hospitals (there are two other hospitals in Katonah, New York, and Chicago) were drawn to Saratoga Springs partly because of its history as a health resort.

73-82, Photographer unknown. Original photograph from the Durkee Collection, 1875

The Civil War Monument, first located on Broadway but moved into Congress Park in 1921, was dedicated on September 21, 1875, to the men from Saratoga who served in the 77th New York Infantry, known as the Bemis Heights Regiment. They left Saratoga for Washington on Thanksgiving Day in 1861 and served in the major battles of the East. Saratogians also served in the 30th and 115th New York Infantry, the 2nd Veteran Cavalry, the 54th Massachusetts Colored Infantry and the 13th New York Heavy Artillery.

Before the Civil war, visitors to Saratoga Springs were often Southerners who came to partake of the waters. During the Civil War, the Saratoga racetrack opened. It began slowly because of the shortage of horses, but after the war ended in 1865, it became a major attraction, and the clientele shifted to wealthy Northerners.

70-119/2, H.G. Brown, Photographer, 1887

The Saratoga Citizens Corps was kept at the ready during their annual inspection in Woodlawn Park (Judge Henry Hilton's estate on North Broadway). Many of Saratoga's well-known families had young men in the Citizen Corps who served in the Spanish-American War. James Westcott Lester was the major commanding the 3rd Battalion, 2nd Regiment, New York Volunteers.

In another photograph of "The Honor Roll" of the Company, the names of all the officers and privates are listed. It states that they were organized March 25, 1878, and that they departed from Saratoga Springs May 2, 1898, at 6:20 a.m., arriving at Camp Black, Hempstend L. I. at 5:05 p.m., on same day.

56-16/A, Photographer unknown, 1898

Most of the lives that were lost in the Spanish-American War were lost to Typhoid and Yellow Fever in dirty camps rather than in fighting. Here the Company L, Second New York Volunteer Infantry was in Tampa, Florida, in June of 1898.

Standing in the back row, left to right, are: F. Brazee, J. Gillis, W. Lee, J. Sweeney, J. Swartwout, G. Foster, C. Dobbin, A. Greenough, G. Dowd, S. Bush, B. Walbridge, H. Todd, R. Miller, O. Wells, T. Pierce, and E. St. John. Standing in the next to back row are: L. Rich, E. Potter, O. Welch, W. Flynn, F. Russell, W. McNaughton, G. Ingalls, R. Ditmar, W. French, J. Walbridge, F. Paul, F. Carpenter, J. A'Hearn, W. Winchester, G. Bannister, C. Gibbs, C. Lockhart, C. Baker, H. Simpson, J. Monahan, F. Pennoyer, E. Durkee, G. Ramsey, B. Burrows, and A. Franklin. Seated are: J. McGhan, F. Clements, D. Epler, H. Thomas, H. Wildey, E. Spaulding, A. Schwarte, F. Burd, Major Lester, Captain Rich, Lieutenant J. Schwarte, Lieutenant O. Coleman, W. Town, R. Parker, F. Ritchie, F. McNair, H. Jamison, J. Miner, W. Searing, W. Waterbury, G. Schmidt, and J. Morris. In the front row, reclining, are: L. Follett, R. Mingay, F. Dunson, C. Fryer, T. Mabee, H. Olmstead, W. Wells, E. Arnold, H. Morris, E.Hays, A. Case, R. Dennin, S. Ostrander, B. Gerberg, and F. Calkins.

83-87, J. S. Wooley, Photographer, 1917
Old veterans, from the Civil War, escorted young recruits on their way to fight in World War I. They marched on Broadway which was lined with flag-waving citizens.

1814, H. B. Settle, Photographer, 1912
On Friday October 18, 1912, the parade of over two thousand people that preceded the dedication exercises of the Saratoga Battle Monument was "one of the most elaborate ever given in northern New York." Headlines in the Saratogian stated, "Governor Dix and Distinguished Company Participate in Exercises—Five Hundred School Children Sing America, Accompanied by Music of Massed Bands—Addresses and Parades Features of the Day-Culmination of Week of Historic Observances and Entertainments." It continued, "At the foot of the Saratoga Battle Monument, towering high above the field of conflict where, one hundred and thirty-five years ago, the battle of Saratoga was fought and won, exercises were held this afternoon formally transferring the structure, erected in commemoration of that struggle, to the State of New York.

The ball this evening will be open to the public free of charge . . . full dress will be necessary for those wishing to dance, but will not be required for those attending the reception or who are among the onlookers."

3530/2, H. B. Settle, Photographer, 1916
Company L, surrounded by family and townspeople, boarded the train at the station on Railroad Place in Saratoga Springs. They were leaving to be part of the fighting in World War I.

9555/6, H. B. Settle, Photographer, 1940

Before the United States entered World War II, various groups raised money to assist the war effort in a "Bundles for Britain" campaign. The British-American Ambulance Corps parked an ambulance at the racetrack. Jockeys, trainers and celebrities all joined in the fundraising campaign. Joe E. Brown and Mrs. W. G. Cavanaugh of New York City deposited money through the back window of the ambulance. Brown was in Saratoga Springs to star in a production at the Spa Little Theater.

10-711/2, H. B. Settle, Photographer, 1944

Saratoga High School joined in the World War II effort during a War Bond Parade on Broadway. Addison Mallery, who was mayor at that time, wrote in a reminiscence to Martha Stonequist, City Historian, about the event. He stated that he and John Quilty went to Newman's and Riley's nightclubs to ask some of the stars to perform. In spite of a microphone breakdown, Gracie Fields helped the cause by singing her famous Aspidistra song.

10.269, H. B. Settle, Photographer, 1943

Members of the Gurtler Brothers Post 420, Veterans of Foreign Wars of the U.S., swore in Ernest C. Hooker, motor mechanic 2nd class, U.S. Navy, who served aboard USS Kilauea. He was the second veteran of World War II to be accepted.

The Gurtler Brother Post 420 was chartered on May 24, 1920, with thirty members. It was named in honor of Corp. William Gurtler and Pvt. George Gurtler, Jr., who were killed in action in 1918 on the Hindenberg Line while serving with Headquarters Company, 105th Infantry, 27th Division.

In this photograph, left to right, are: Pietro Mastropasqua, Post Commander John Butler, Florence Cunningham (Hooker's sister), Auxiliary President Mary Parmatier, past Council Commander Joseph Cunningham, Ernest Hooker, Howard Cook, District Auxiliary President Grace Cook, Arthur Parmatier and Jacob Aison.

10.252, H. B. Settle, Photographer, 1943

During World War II, air raid wardens were part of the home defense effort. Skidmore students with arm bands of the "U.S. Army Air Force, Observer," took their turns as wardens for the school. Addison Mallery, as mayor during World War II, had the responsibility of ensuring total blackout of the city in case of enemy bombing. From the top of the Grand Union Hotel, which can be seen in the background of this photograph, the entire city could be viewed and any cracks of light checked out.

72-46, Photographer unknown, circa 1860

    Before the Civil war many visitors from the South frequented Saratoga Springs. Here a group of them posed by the Columbian Spring in Congress Park. During the later part of the Victorian era, this structure was taken down to be replaced by a more decorative pavilion. Eventually the Congress and the Columbian pavilions were joined into one large springhouse with stained glass windows and ornate woodwork. A replica of this original springhouse now stands in Congress Park.

D71-28, H.B. Settle, Photographer.

Postcard Graphics Artist unknown. 1915
In this photograph, taken for a postcard, a
group of people were partaking of Congress
Spring water at the sunken spring in the
foreground. In the background was a
springhouse and the bandstand.

The 1915 Saratoga Directory described
Congress Park: ". . . The City Park includes
what was formerly the Congress Hall Hotel
property, the old Congress Spring Park and
the Canfield Park. The plot of ground is
bounded by Broadway, Spring Street and
Circular Street and contains about ten acres
of ground. It was laid out by Charles W.
Leavitt, Jr., landscape engineer, and
includes several artistic lakes, a stream and
cascade, the beautiful memorial fountain
erected to the memory of the late Spencer
Trask...and also the Italian Gardens, in the
northeast section. In excess of half a million
dollars has been spent in the beautifying and
ornamentation of this charming park. This
sum includes the spacious building which is
now used as a Casino, which was formerly
the noted Canfield place. It is claimed this is
the most beautiful park of its size in the
United States."

W25, J. S. Wooley, Photographer, circa 1900
This was the entrance to Congress Park at the turn of the century.
The Congress and Columbian Spring pavilions were festooned with
lights and flags for a convention. The Civil War Monument, which is
now inside the park, stood on Broadway. In the foreground a newsboy
sold newspapers to people passing by in carriages. In the background
the tower of Convention Hall could be seen and beyond it the roofline
of the Windsor Hotel.

78-21/3, Photographer unknown, 1880
    Deer Spring in Congress Park was named after the Deer Park House, an enclosure for deer, which was at the south end of the park just down from the Batcheller mansion. "Pure Water From Spring Near Deer Park" was written on the front of the spring fountain. It is possible that the spring was tapped near the enclosure and piped to this part of the park. In this area visitors could sit under the trees and enjoy music concerts from one of the two bandstands nearby.

S-3, Photographer unknown, circa 1880
    Two gentlemen sit beside the bandstand in Congress Park.

3742, H. B. Settle, Photographer, 1917

This is Canfield Casino in Congress Park. The round rooms to the left of the side door were small, private dining rooms that are no longer part of the building.

Built by John Morrissey as a gambling establishment in 1870, the Casino was originally known as Morrissey's Club House with an address of 41 East Congress Street which was at the intersection of East Congress and Putnam. At that time Congress Park was smaller and to the south. East Congress Street joined Union Avenue and Putnam Street did not stop at Spring, but ran through to East Congress. Richard Canfield, the "Prince of Gamblers," bought the property in 1894.

The village acquired the property in 1911. By 1913 Congress Hall and the final Club House Lodgings on Putnam Street came down to make the area of Congress Park as we know it today.

1632 detail, H. B. Settle, Photographer, 1912

This is a small detail from a glass-plate negative. The George F. Doring Band from Troy, New York, was performing at the hillside bandstand in Congress Park. Until this detail was discovered and enlarged by Michael Noonan, there was never a picture of the bandstand although George S. Bolster talked about being "dragged" over to it as a child.

City Historian Martha Stonequist was able to find a contract that the village had with George F. Doring for a sum of $388 per week to furnish three daily concerts in Congress Spring Park in 1914. The band included eighteen skilled, uniformed musicians including one flute, one E flat clarinet, three B flat clarinets, three cornets, two French horns, three trombones, one baritone, one bass, two drums and one conductor.

140

126, H. B. Settle, Photographer, 1905

The dining room of Canfield Casino was an addition to the building in 1901. During Richard Canfield's time, it was presided over by a famous French Chef, Jean Columbin. The dining room served gourmet food to patrons and their guests. Although women were not allowed to gamble they could dine at the Casino.

During the 1940s and 1950s the octagonal stained glass windows disappeared and the room fell into disrepair, although it was still used for many city functions. The city undertook a restoration in the mid 1970s. The windows were mysteriously returned and the city hired a restorer, Steven Henderer, who worked for many months to return them to their original condition.

A modern kitchen has been installed beyond the dining room, which today looks very much like this 1905 photograph. It is used for many civic and social functions.

1328, H. B. Settle, Photographer, 1911

Evening clothes were the expected dress in Canfield's Casino. In this public gaming room downstairs, the stakes were from one to one thousand dollars. In the private high-stakes rooms upstairs, the chips were valued from one hundred to one hundred thousand dollars. Women and village residents were not allowed in the gaming rooms. Canfield installed a safe in the downstairs room that currently houses the Historical Society gift shop and the Ann Grey Gallery. The safe apparently held one million dollars in currency.

Although this was the low stakes room, it was elaborately finished with carved woodwork and mirrors. In the room beyond there was a bar and a few tables. Over the years the bar had been removed so during the restoration of the Casino in the 1970s, a reproduction was made and installed with funds raised by the Pillar Society.

3317/2, H. B. Settle, Photographer, 1915

The Italian Gardens in Congress Park were built by Richard Canfield. Canfield purchased the Casino in 1894. By 1901 there was talk of prohibiting gambling in Saratoga Springs and only half a dozen gaming houses were permitted to operate. Canfield decided to beautify the area around his Casino and make it a showplace of which the village would be proud. To do this he purchased land behind and adjacent to the Casino property that held a furniture warehouse (formerly an Academy Bicycle Casino), some of the Club House Lodgings and an Indian Encampment. He had most of the buildings torn down and the area cleared out. By 1903 he had constructed the Italian Gardens to resemble the courtyard of an Italian palace. Despite these efforts, public pressure against gambling continued and Canfield closed the Casino in 1907.

3216, H. B. Settle, Photographer 1915

The Spencer Trask Memorial was commissioned by Katrina Trask, in consultation with George Foster Peabody, as a memorial to her husband. Daniel Chester French was selected as the sculptor. One of America's best known sculptors, he also did the Minuteman in Concord and the Lincoln Memorial in Washington, D.C. The architectural setting for the memorial was done by Henry Bacon. Above the statue of the "Spirit of Life," the words of Governor Hughes are written: "His Chief Aim Was To Do Good and Serve His Fellow Men." The dedication was held on July 14, 1914.

Spencer Trask had become very interested in the waters of Saratoga Springs and was chairman of the New York State Reservation Commission. In 1909 he was traveling to New York City with the Commission's report that was to save the springs from businesses that were illegally pumping great quantities of mineral water to extract carbonic gas. His train was in a collision and he was killed.

87-31/6, Michael L. Noonan, Photographer, 1987

The Historical Society of Saratoga Springs has operated a museum in Canfield Casino since 1912. A major exhibit is the recreation of a Victorian parlor from the H. C. Todd House, featuring an outstanding collection of rosewood furniture by the master cabinetmaker Henry Belter.

4790/A, H. B. Settle, Photographer, 1922

"And the band plays on" in this idyllic scene from Congress Park. The original bandstand was a graceful structure with thin columns and decorative ironwork. Band concerts were common during the season with the village contracting with various bands to supply music in the two locations in the park.

Although later photographs show that it was still in good condition, the city decided to replace this bandstand with a war memorial. The cornerstone for the memorial was laid May 22, 1931. The memorial contains monuments to veterans of World War I and II and the Korean and Vietnam wars.

4766A, H. B. Settle, Photographer, 1922

Several hundred citizens gathered for the presentation of the Katrina Trask Gateway to Congress Park on November 15, 1922. At the presentation, George Foster Peabody gave an address stating "... the citizens of Saratoga Springs have kept green the memory of Commissioner Trask about the noble memory enshrining the Spirit of Life, one of the finest and most beautiful examples of modern statuary .... It is fitting that this beautiful park should also have a memorial to the Lady of Yaddo, as her fellow citizens have called her with true affection." (The Saratogian November 16, 1922)

70-120, Photographer unknown, circa 1919

Joe S. "Old Pop" Nickerson, known as the philosopher of Saratoga Lake, had this stand at the end of the trolley line at Saratoga Lake. He had come to Saratoga Springs in 1901, pitched a tent at the side of the road and continued to do business at this wayside stand of the "Walled Off Astoria" every summer for nineteen years. "Pop" was known to everyone in Saratoga. On his birthday, April 1, he would write a letter full of common-sense philosophy to the children of Saratoga Springs. It was published in the Saratogian annually. His philosophy of life was "Be good and do good." He had a pet pig and a guitar. He entertained and sold refreshments to people waiting for the trolley back into town from Saratoga Lake.

4239/3, H. B. Settle, Photographer, 1922

A thrilling water slide dominated the swimming and boating beach at Kaydeross Park on Saratoga Lake. The park was first listed in the Saratoga Directory in 1900 with Saratoga Traction Company as the proprietor. By 1905 it was owned by the Hudson Valley Railroad. Their trolleys ran to the lake and people flocked to swim and enjoy the water during the hot days of summer. Only four miles from Saratoga Springs, Saratoga Lake has always played an important part in the history of the city. The Mohawk Indians called it "Caniaderiossera" and believed its stillness was sacred to the Great Spirit and that no words could be spoken while they were in canoes on its surface.

2973/1, H. B. Settle, Photographer, 1915

Ice harvesting was a major industry on Saratoga Lake. Ice was stored under sawdust in sheds, and was used to keep the hotels and homes of Saratoga supplied all summer. The 1919 Saratoga Directory stated that this business was owned by the Grippin family who also owned a large grocery store at the corner of Caroline and Henry streets.

78-67, Photographer unknown, circa 1875

White Sulphur Springs Hotel, Springs and Baths were located on the east shore of Saratoga Lake about a mile south of Snake Hill and about eight miles from Saratoga Springs. The hotel was built in the early 1870s and torn down in 1957. In her book *Saratoga, Queen of the Spas*, Grace Swanner, M.D., writes of the spring. ". . . it lies in a beautiful ravine through which runs a small stream which is fed by fresh water springs. The course of the spring to the brook is marked by a deposit of sulphur. The water is strongly charged with sulphureited hydrogen." Today a deteriorated rustic springhouse still stands at the side of the road.

White Sulphur Springs advertised a new and complete hotel for a hundred guests, broad piazzas, a 150 acre park, fish and game dinners and a bathhouse. A horse-drawn omnibus line left Saratoga Springs and returned regularly throughout the day.

The steamboat in the background of the photograph was the Lady of the Lake. It went to Briggs House, a hotel at the north end of the lake and back. Passengers could take the omnibus and steamboat ride for a dollar round-trip from Saratoga Springs. The Lady of the Lake was brought overland from the Hudson River. When it was due to be replaced, it was sunk in the deep water off Snake Hill. To this day people claim to be able to see it when the water is calm or, in the winter, when the ice is clear.

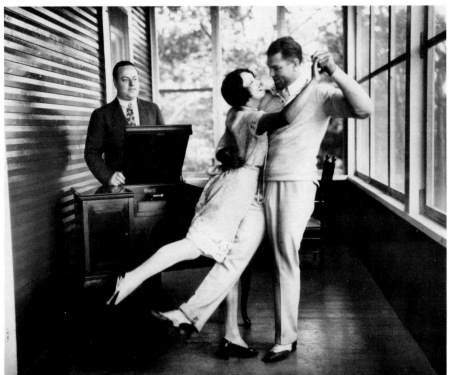

5605/3, H. B. Settle, Photographer, 1926

On a porch at White Sulphur Springs Hotel, Jack Dempsey, world champion heavyweight prizefighter, and his second wife, actress Estelle Taylor, danced between practice sessions. Both Jack Dempsey and Jean Tunney trained at this Saratoga Lake hotel. There was a boxing ring with seats at the side of the lake where Saratogians and visitors to the area could watch sparring matches.

Harlan Page stood behind his product, the Brunswick Phonograph (Victrola). In 1923 Page had a store, at the northeast corner of Caroline Street and Maple Avenue, which dealt with phonographs, records, pianos and sewing machines. The business also did hemstitching and Picot edge work. By 1928 his store was Harlan Page Music Store Company at 350 Broadway.

81-08, Photographer unknown, 1909

"The Apollo Club at Saratoga Lake — 09" was written on the negative by an unknown photographer. A sign on the building says "The Claredon," which might indicate that Clarendon Hotel in Saratoga Springs had a cottage at Saratoga Lake.

9437, H. B. Settle, Photographer, 1940

One of the earliest lake houses was Riley's, opened by James and Hanna Riley in the mid 1800s. Fish and game dinners, boating and bathing made it a popular destination for the late afternoon carriage parade from Saratoga Springs.

Destroyed by fire in the early 1930s, Riley's was totally rebuilt in the art deco style shown in this photograph. The lobby was a twenty-four-foot octagonal space decorated in black, silver and gold. A large staff was required to handle the restaurant. Gambling and top-line entertainment kept customers coming to the lake until the 1950s investigation by U.S. Sen. Estes Kefauver forced gambling establishments to close.

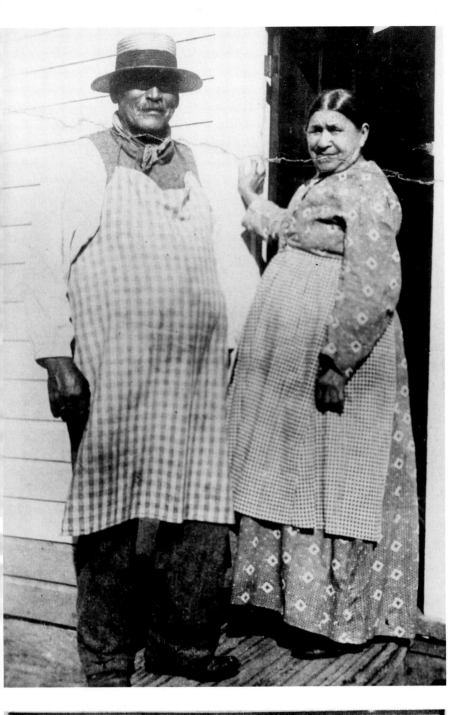

73-57, Photographer unknown, circa 1860

As Riley's lake house lured more and more people to Saratoga Lake each season, rival lake houses sprang up. One of the most popular of these was opened by Cary B. Moon in 1853. Tending the kitchen at Moon's were George Crum (Speck) and "Aunt Kate" Wicks his sister and assistant. George Crum was a Native American with Spanish and German blood, who had learned to be an incomparable fish and game cook while working as a guide in the Adirondacks. Eventually he opened his own restaurant on Saratoga Lake. It became a favorite of William H. Vanderbilt and other socialites who went to him in ". . . swarms, droves and flocks and were turned away by the score hour after hour, because he could not feed them all. His rules of procedure were his own. They were very strict, and being an Indian, he never departed from them. In the slang of the race-course he 'played no favorites'. Guests were obliged to wait their turn, the millionaire as well as the wage earner. Mr. Vanderbilt was once obliged to wait an hour and a half for a meal." (N.Y. Tribune, December 27, 1891)

77-07, George S. Bolster, Photographer. Michael L. Noonan, Assistant Photographer, Photograph 1977, box date circa 1860

Stories abound about the invention of the Saratoga Chip, the first name of the potato chip as we know it today. Evelyn Barrett Britten, who was the first city historian from 1923 to 1925 and again from 1947 to 1969 wrote about the matter in the Chronicles of Saratoga in 1959: ". . . history must record that a trio produced the potato chip which has grown to fame and still flourishes. The trio includes 'Aunt Katie' Wicks, George Crum, (Speck) and Cary B. Moon. 'Aunt Katie', as she was familiarly known by friends and patrons of the popular Moon's Lakehouse at Saratoga Lake where she worked as a cook, was in the kitchen in mid-July 1853. She was baking crullers and had a pan of deep fat on the stove nearby, while at the same time, she was peeling potatoes. Suddenly she chipped off a piece of potato, which by the merest accident fell into the pan of fat. She fished it out with her long fork and put it down on the plate beside her on the table. She went on with her work of peeling, when her brother, George Crum, came into the kitchen. 'What's this?' he asked after he had picked up the chip and tasted it. 'Hm, Hm, that's good, how did you make it?' he asked his sister. 'Make it,' she said, astounded 'it was just an accident'. And she described what had happened. 'It's a good accident,' said Crum. 'We'll have plenty of these.'" There are many versions of this story, one involving Mr. Vanderbilt, who sent back some potatoes that he did not like. Crum threw pieces of them into hot oil. The only thing that people agree upon is the fact that the potato chip was invented at Moon's Lakehouse by George Crum and his sister Katie.

147

65-150/16, *Probably taken by Harrison Epler, circa 1875. Later mounted on mount board of Epler and Arnold, Photographers (1887-1897).*

College regattas were held on Saratoga Lake each summer from 1871 through 1876. In a column "Turn Back the Pages" in the Saratogian on July 11, 1985, former City Historian Bea Sweeney describes "the greatest intercollegiate regatta ever held in the United States" at Saratoga Lake on July 14, 1875. "The sky was hazy blue, the lake had only a few ripples and the 25,000 people crowded into the grandstand on Ramsdill's Point, the surrounding beach and woods, waited for the race to begin . . . . Amherst, Bowdoin, Brown, Columbia, Cornell, Dartmouth, Hamilton, Harvard, Princeton, Union, Wesleyan, Williams and Yale each had separate quarters at various spots around the lake. The Saratoga Rowing Association had even constructed housing, complete with raft and flag staff for the scull of each crew. The three mile straight away started just north of Snake Hill and ended in the Ramsdill's Point area. Lanes were 100 feet wide marked with colorful flags each one-eighth mile."

Cornell won. It took two hours for the crew to reach town where the freshman crew carried the heavyweight winners triumphantly up the stairs of the United States Hotel. Trophies and other awards were presented later at a ceremony in Congress Hall.

Races at Saratoga Lake are a tradition that has recently been revived, spearheaded by the Skidmore College Rowing Association.

W85, *J. S. Wooley, Photographer, circa 1900*

Newman's was another famous Saratoga lake house that catered to the late afternoon carriage parade from Saratoga Springs. The broad verandas and simple structure were typical of lake houses. At the turn of the century visitors came to enjoy the country air and rural vistas followed by fish and game dinners. Later, Newman's changed into a restaurant with a nightclub and gambling rooms. It was razed in 1972.

9882/3, H. B. Settle, Photographer, 1941
New York Telephone Company employees enjoyed a party at Newman's lake house in 1941. Photographs of the interiors of lake houses are quite rare except for party pictures like this or empty rooms that were taken for New York State liquor licensing.

6090/3, H. B. Settle, Photographer, 1928
In 1928 the B.P.O.E. (Elks Club) held their clambake at the Arrowhead, another lake house which burned down in 1969. This photograph is from one of many badly deteriorated negatives in the George S. Bolster Collection. The edges were cut off to prevent further deterioration and a print was made of the center of the image.

82-09/4, Photographer unknown, circa 1865

High Rock Spring was the first of the mineral springs discovered in this region. It had been used by Native Americans for medicinal purposes. Although missionaries and explorers probably visited in the 1760s, the Native Americans brought Sir William Johnson on a stretcher to the spring in 1771, making him the first known white man to visit this area. The history of the spring is long and varied. After a variety of owners had built crude accommodations, Alexander Bryan finally purchased the property in 1787 and erected a blacksmith shop and log cabin which he operated as a tavern. In 1783 George Washington attempted to purchase the spring after a visit as the guest of General Schuyler.

When Seymour Ainsworth and W. H. McCaffrey retubed the spring in 1865, they found evidence of very early Native American use. They erected a springhouse with a mosque-like dome crowned by an immense golden eagle. By 1872 they were bankrupt and the spring was sold at auction for sixteen thousand dollars. The Saratoga High Rock Spring Company was formed and ran the operation until 1904.

A few years later the property was purchased by the village of Saratoga Springs to be maintained as a park under an agreement with the Saratoga Springs Reservation Commission. The village owned the property and New York State owned the spring rights.

The original land was swampy and wet and subject to flooding by the village brook, as can be seen in this picture. A filling operation raised the land so the large cone depicted in early drawings seemed sunken and small later.

In this photograph the High Rock Pavilion with the dome and golden eagle rises beyond the swampy lake-like area. There was a bottling plant behind the spring and various other structures were situated along the High Rock Spring escarpment.

S-39, Photographer unknown, circa 1880

High Rock Spring is described in *Saratoga, Queen of the Spas*, by Grace Swanner, M.D., as "... covered by a unique conical structure, resembling a miniature volcano, composed of tufa or travertine, which is a deposit of carbonates laid down from water as it flowed over the top of the mound, as it was known to do in earlier days. The carbonates come out of solution from the water as carbon dioxide gas, which made the water acid, was released. As long as the water is underground and under pressure, the carbon dioxide gas stays in the water, but when it reaches the surface of the earth where pressure is reduced, it is given off from the water in the form of bubbles. Over the years carbonates have formed at the mouth of the spring, forming the mound and embedding the sticks and other material in it. The cone is 37 inches in height and 25.6 inches in circumference at the base. On the summit there is a circular aperture 10 inches in diameter."

3225, H. B. Settle, photographer, 1915

Originally this building housed the Magnetic Spring Baths which were discovered in 1873 by William P. Slocum. In *Saratoga, Queen of the Spas*, Grace Swanner, M.D. states, "It was claimed that the Magnetic Bath House was the only one in Saratoga Springs that had porcelain-lined tubs, a steam boiler and electric bells. The spring ceased to flow and was filled up in 1914." It was located on Spring Avenue (now High Rock Avenue) and advertised in the Saratoga Directory as a spring used for diseases peculiar to women.

In 1915 the Magnetic Bath House became the High Rock Spring Baths, using High Rock water. By 1918 the bathhouse was condemned and was demolished. The following year work was begun in the larger Washington Bath House and the emphasis of the Spa shifted from High Rock Park.

78-65, Photographer unknown, circa 1870

Visitors thronged Seltzer and High Rock springs which were located on Spring Avenue (now High Rock Avenue). Described in the 1871 Saratoga Directory, Seltzer Spring ". . . formerly called 'Barrel Spring' because a barrel was used for tubing, is near High Rock Spring. The ground about the spring was wet and the spring was suffered to pass out of notice. In 1860 Dr. Haslans purchased the lot containing the spring and began the work of excavating with thirty men. A shaft twenty by thirty feet was excavated through five feet of muck, four of tufa, twenty-one of blue clay and four of hardpan, down to the calciferous sand rock. A birch tree eighteen inches in diameter and thirty feet long, with portions of the roots attached, was found in the calciferous deposit. The spring was substantially tubed and in 1868 a bottling house was erected." The High Rock Spring house, with the large eagle on top of the building, was located to the north of the Seltzer Spring.

3223, H. B. Settle, Photographer, 1915

Emperor Spring was located near the Seltzer Spring, just south of High Rock. At this time, Emperor was reached by going down steps to the spring. Two factors may account for this. First, the area was marshy and fill had been brought in to raise the level of the valley. Second, the overpumping of the waters by the carbonic gas companies had seriously depleted the strength of flow of the springs. Emperor was retubed in 1916 and brought back to a pure condition. It was one of the most popular of the springs as is evidenced by the number of visitors in this photograph.

70-119/1, Baker and Record, Photographers, circa 1870

Pavilion Spring was located off Lake Avenue, behind the Pavilion Hotel, which stood where City Hall is today. The Pavilion Hotel was built by Nathan Lewis and opened on May 26, 1819. It had a two-story front and a one-story piazza which ran the length of the front of the building. There was a large wing which was on Lake Avenue. The landscaped ground reached to Grove Street.

The spring itself was tubed in 1839 by Daniel McLaren who had bought the Pavilion Hotel in 1832. In 1871 it was owned by the Pavilion and United States Spring Company. The Saratoga Directory of that year stated ". . . they have greatly improved the surroundings, laying out walks and shade trees."

70-119/4, Photographer unknown, circa 1880

This spring, located north of High Rock Spring, had many names over the years. Originally it was called Gunpowder Spring because of its odor. In 1784 it was President Spring. In 1793 it was Walton Spring for its owner Jacob Walton. When it was tubed in 1834 and was found to contain Iodine, it became Iodine Spring. In the 1871 Saratoga Directory it is listed as: "Saratoga Star Spring formerly called Saline Spring." The Saratoga Star Spring Company acquired it in 1865. By 1878 the Directory could say, ". . . it was first known 30 years ago, has greatly increased its popularity and universally recognized as one of the leading waters of the many springs found at Saratoga. Office and bottling house at the spring. L. A. Pratt, superintendent."

3189, H. B. Settle, Photographer, 1915

The New York State Reservation Commission was formed in 1909 to protect the springs from depletion by private gas companies which were pumping huge amounts of water to extract the gasses from them. The gas was in demand at soda fountains across the country. In her book Saratoga, Queen of the Spas, Grace M. Swanner, M.D., talks about Hathorn No. 1: "The building was painted inside and out in white trimmed with green. A large multiple drinking fountain thirty-four feet in diameter and four feet high was installed. It was designed so that a number of people at a time could fill their glasses with different mineral waters. It was capable of serving twenty-four

people a minute . . . . About the hall were tables and chairs to accommodate a hundred people at a time. A fee of five cents was charged for admission to the hall. Hathorn #1 water was served from a double fountain; one side of which supplied water inside the drink hall; the other side, separated by an ornamental partition, supplied the water free of charge to people outside at the spring."

The Hathorn No. 1 Pavilion was located on the northwest corner of Spring Street at Putnam. Today a small springhouse is on the site. This spring was discovered when the foundation for the Congress Hall ballroom was being excavated.

8713, H. B. Settle, Photographer, 1937

On Saturday afternoon May 1, 1937, fire struck the Hathorn No. 1 drink hall, which was a State Reservation building. People were evacuated from the surrounding buildings. Donald Mercer recalled that he was one of a number of children attending the Saturday afternoon matinee at the Congress Theater who were escorted out of the movie theater. The Reservation building was heavily damaged and subsequently torn down.

57-64/5, Photographer unknown, circa 1893

On the left-hand side of this photograph, looking down Phila Street from Broadway, were Whealey's Market and the Saratoga Baths. These baths were advertised in the 1909 Saratoga Directory as ". . . the finest baths in America: Turkish, Russian, Roman, Mineral, Plain and Swimming Baths. The value of the Old Putnam Mineral Spring Water Baths as a curative medium in cases of Rheumatism,

Indigestion, Skin Diseases, Nervousness, etc., cannot be overestimated. H. M. Levengston, proprietor."

Apparently the waters for this bathhouse came from the original Putnam Spring. On the right-hand side of the photograph were Fassett Paint Store and then the Patterson Spring. This spring was discovered in 1886 on the property of Alexander H. Patterson.

154

220/2, H. B. Settle, Photographer, 1906

The interior of the Patterson Spring Drink Hall had forty-foot-high ceilings and was very popular dispensing water to fifteen-hundred to two thousand people daily. In 1893 it advertised in the Saratoga Directory: "This is a new spring that in Cathartic, Alternative and Effervesent Qualities is Unrivalled and its Result is called 'Wonderful'. The Spring Pavilion is the Most Elegant in the Village and being so pleasantly located is a proper resort of visitors at Saratoga."

78-13, Photographer unknown, circa 1860

Hamilton Spring was located on the southeast corner of Putnam and Spring Street in an area that is now Congress Park. In the background a dipper-boy stood ready to dip water for gentlemen visitors in this pre-Civil War era. This spring was discovered and tubed by Gideon Putnam in 1809. He had built a bathhouse just north of Congress Spring which he later moved to Hamilton Spring. The sign for the bathhouse was prominently displayed on the side of the springhouse.

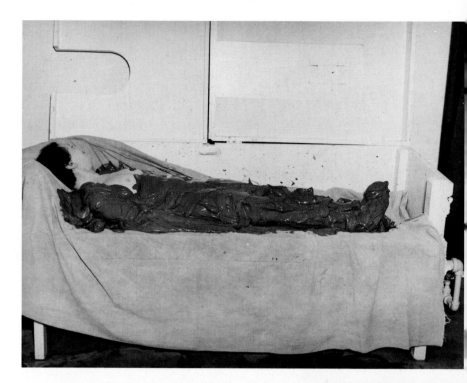

8728, H. B. Settle, Photographer, 1937

The new bathhouses on the Spa Reservation offered the most up-to-date therapies. The tubs were made of material impervious to carbon dioxide gas with polished stainless steel fixtures. The services offered in addition to the baths were: steam rooms, electric light cabinet rooms, hot rooms, vichy douches, infra red and ultra violet, diathermy treatments, inhalation, mechanotherapy, mudpacks, salt rubs and massages.

79-16, Photographer unknown, circa 1860

In this charming photograph, the Excelsior Spring carriage and a private carriage had arrived at the spring. The Excelsior and Union springs were located in the Valley of the Ten Spring Woods about a mile from town hall. The waters ". . . are put up in pint and quart bottles and packed in good order for shipment to any part of the world. Pints in boxes of four dozen each, and quarts in boxes of two dozen each. They are also shipped in Lawrences Patent Reservoirs (barrels lined with pure tin) from which they are dispensed by our customers at their counters precisely as they flow from the springs, without being recharged with gas." (1883 Saratoga Directory) Excelsior Spring Water, a "sweet" non-carbonated water, is now bottled on the site by the Excelsior Springs Water Company.

4239/7, H. B. Settle, Photographer, 1919

Cars lined the driveway in front of the Washington Baths in this photograph made from a deteriorated 1919 negative. The building was the primary hydrotherapy facility at the Spa until 1930 when the new Lincoln Bathhouse was built. In 1938 the Washington Baths were updated and a heating system installed. In the following years the Washington Baths underwent extensive redecoration, but by the 1960s hydrotherapy had become unpopular and this bathhouse closed in 1978.

A readaptive use was found for the building in 1986 when it became home to the National Museum of Dance. Under the auspices of the Saratoga Performing Arts Center and a separate Board of Directors, chaired by Lewis A. Swyer and Mrs. Cornelius Vanderbilt Whitney, who spearheaded fundraising activities, the Museum opened on July 7, 1986. By 1987 there were two temporary and one permanent exhibit "Shaping the American Dance Dream" housed in the Dance Hall of Fame. The Hall of Fame is dedicated to Mr. and Mrs. C. V. Whitney and honors founders of American Dance.

Further expansion is planned and the museum will become home to the New York State School of Dance sponsored by the State Education Department and the Saratoga Performing Arts Center.

8662, H. B. Settle, Photographer, 1937

June 5, 1930, was the dedication day for the new $750,000 Lincoln Bath House. It was the beginning of what was to make Saratoga Springs a great mecca of health. The building was the largest bathhouse in the world under one roof, capable of forty-five hundred treatments per day. Busses ran from the city to bring patrons to the baths.

Initially the Saratoga Springs Reservation had only three bathhouses: The Lincoln and the Washington were in Lincoln Park on the Reservation at the southern edge of the city and the Saratoga Bath House on Phila Street. At this point the New York State legislature had appropriated a million dollars to develop the Saratoga Spa. In the early 1930s, James M. Friedlander, an architect, went to Europe with Bernard Baruch to study health spas. After this trip he drew the plans for the development of Geyser Park.

66-61, Photographer unknown, circa 1880

The Saratoga Vichy Spring was drilled in 1872 and, because its composition resembled the Vichy Spring in France, it was named Saratoga Vichy. The Saratoga Directory of 1878 said it ". . . is beautifully located on Ballston Avenue, west of the railroad on the bank of a placid little lake, and poetically set in an iron fountain under a picturesque pavilion. The water is brought from its source to the surface—180 feet—in glass lined tubing and takes special rank among the valuable mineral waters of this famous spa. Office and bottling house at the spring."

In 1902 the French government brought a suit against the Saratoga Vichy Spring Company charging that they did not have the right to the name Vichy. The case ended when the Supreme Court decided in favor of the Saratoga Vichy Spring Company which had been using the name for over twenty-five years.

Saratoga Water is bottled on the same site today by the Saratoga Springs Mineral Water Company with a parent company in France.

3222, H. B. Settle, Photographer, 1915

This rustic porch was used as a breakfast room at the Geyser Spring bottling house.

All the water that was bottled was analyzed for its mineral and gas content and checked regularly for purity. On September 14, 1934, Governor Lehman announced that the newly constructed laboratory and research building would be named the Simon Baruch Research Laboratory in honor of the father of Bernard Baruch. Simon Baruch had been an early supporter and promoter of the springs at Saratoga.

6165 detail, H. B. Settle, Photographer, 1929

This is a center detail from a badly deteriorated negative. It shows Hayes Well at the Geysers. In the foreground, a group of animated visitors around the well were watched by a lone woman sitting on the steps. Behind this group a man lounged on the grass beside a table which advertised "Chicken Dinner 5 cents."

549, H. B. Settle, Photographer, 1908

Carbonic acid gas was in great demand during the Victorian era for use in soda fountains and in refrigeration. In 1908 the New York State legislature passed an anti-pumping act after it was determined that pumping at any of the springs and wells lessened the force of gas and the flow of water in all others. The gas companies fought this bill. Newspapers, including the Saratogian, the New York Journal of Medicine and the Wall Street Journal argued in favor of state ownership of the springs. The anti-pumping bill was fought to the U.S. Supreme Court which finally ruled it was constitutional.

This photograph shows a carbonic gas company with its collecting unit. There are many other photographs in the collection which show the gas tanks and valves that were used for shipping.

8483/A, H. B. Settle, Photographer, 1936

This was the interior of the Saratoga Vichy bottling plant. The name can be seen on a wooden case next to the male employee on the far right of the photograph.

Probably the first bottler of water in Saratoga Springs was John Clarke around 1823. He purchased Congress Spring and, in partnership with Thomas Lynch, built a bottling plant next to the spring. He had owned a successful soda fountain business in New York City and became very successful selling his bottled water throughout the United States and Europe.

Over the years bottled water became a big business with most of the major springs bottling and distributing water. This photograph was taken for the Saratoga Springs Authority in 1936.

7480/2, H. B. Settle, Photographer, 1933

The cornerstone of the Hall of Springs, a building designed by Joseph Friedlander, was laid July 12, 1933. Dignitaries present were Pierport B. Noyes, chairman of the Reservation Commission; Gov. Herbert H. Lehman, who gave the principal address and Mr. Bernard Baruch, who presided over a Masonic ritual of the laying of the cornerstone. The inscription at the Hall of Springs read "In this favored spot spring waters of life that heal the maladies of man and cheer his heart."

57-134, Photographer unknown, circa 1897

Proud of their engine (No. 213 of the Delaware & Hudson Railroad) which was decorated for the Floral fete, these trainmen stood at the Division Street crossing, next to the railway station on Railroad Place. Buildings on Franklin Square can be seen in the background. Notice the Chaplin-like policeman in the left of the photograph.

81-33/2, Photographer unknown, circa 1897

In this floral fete parade, Rev. Mr. Gesser and Mrs. Gesser of the Second Presbyterian Church were in the carriage of Lucy Scribner. The Scribner House at 791 North Broadway is in the background.

In the 1885 Saratoga Directory there was a listing for a "School Garden of Floral Festival Association. Judson A. Lewis, Supt. Broadway adjoining Convention Hall." It went on to state that the "Floral Festival Association holds its annual meeting for the election of officers in June. The street parade and battle of the flowers will be held hereafter annually on two or more days about the first week of September."

Many of the flowers used to decorate the carriages were grown by John Ralph, who had greenhouses at 275 Woodlawn Avenue.

2288 detail, H. B. Settle, Photographer, 1913

Groups of people, all in costume, gathered in Congress Park to participate in the 1913 pageant, held from July 28 to August 2. The pageant brochure stated there were twenty-five hundred in the cast, which depicted historical scenes from the seventeenth-century departure of the Dutch for Manhattan to the return of Civil War troops to Saratoga Springs.

2247, H. B. Settle, Photographer, 1913

The pageant held in Congress Park in 1913 was an elaborate affair with costumes made in great detail. This photograph shows the "Officers' Surrender." At the turn of the century many people were entertained by participating in and watching pageants. Stands were erected in Congress Park for both spectators and a choir.

161

2250, H. B. Settle, Photographer, 1913
   A group of young women took part in the 1913
pageant performing the "Maize Dance."

960, H. B. Settle, Photographer, 1910

The Masons have had three homes in Saratoga Springs. The third floor of the Starbuck Building (at 408-412 Broadway) was the home of the Masonic Temple when this photograph was taken in 1910. The group purchased and moved to the House of Pansa, which they used for thirty years before moving to their present location at 687 North Broadway.

1132, H. B. Settle, Photographer, 1911

On Wednesday February 22, 1911, the Saratogian announced the patrons and patronesses of the The Butterflies, a play to be presented at the Broadway Theater (in Town Hall) by members of the Comedy Club for the benefit of local charities.

In a review of Henry Guy Carleton's play the Saratogian said, "The Butterflies is no parlor dramatics play. It is not the slapstick, funny-situation-every-minute style of play which practically produces itself. There is a lot of opportunity for character work . . ." It continues, "The audience was enthusiastic from first to last curtain. Wives, husbands, fathers, mothers, sweethearts and friends applauded and laughed and applauded some more."

The theater was on the second floor of Town Hall and was complete with footlights, eight painted scenic panels and a green room. Charles Brackett received his start in the Comedy Club and later went on to become a famous Hollywood producer and director. When the theater was torn out of City Hall during the Depression, several advertising posters were found which revealed that Sarah Bernhardt, Robert Martell, Charles Froham, David Belasco, Pat Rooney and Chauncey Olcott, among others, had appeared on stage here.

11-841, H. B. Settle, Photographer, 1947

In the 1940s, radio was an important part of entertainment in the country. WGY, developed by the General Electric Company in Schenectady was a pioneer radio station, and "Farm Paper of the Air" was one of their most popular programs.

Here they were broadcasting from the ballroom of the Grand Union Hotel during a convention. Above the stage in the ballroom was a large crystal chandelier and behind the guest speakers was the painting The Genius of America by the French artist Aldolphe Yuon. This painting almost covered the entire west wall of the room. In a copy of the hotel brochure of 1950, it was described as depicting "America, represented by a beautiful woman of Amazonian stature and proportions, dispensing from a huge 'Horn of Plenty' learning, culture, healing and largess generally, to the assembled nations of the world." The painting now hangs in the New York State Education Department in Albany.

Spa Theater, George S. Bolster, Photographer, 1959

In the 1940s and 1950s, the Saratoga Spa "Little Theater" was one of the most popular stages in the country for summer stock productions. At that time, all the greats of the theater toured in summer to bring plays and entertainment to rural America. George Bolster chronicled these productions by setting his Linhof camera on a step in the upper section of the theater where the camera was at stage level. He would take pictures of the actual productions with existing light. Working late into the night, he would develop and print the photographs, then take them to the Worden Hotel Bar or the Colonial Tavern where the cast and director had gathered. They made selections for themselves, for playbills at the theater and for the display board at the Public Library.

In this photograph, Groucho Marx was starring in Time for Elizabeth, July 13, 1959. Groucho Marx was so impressed by George Bolster's work that he had him come to the Sacandaga Theater to take publicity shots. Whenever the photographs were used, Marx would have the clippings sent to the Bolster studio at 1 Phila Street.

165

50-331/3, Charles C. Hutchins, Photographer, 1950

The Tiger Club was a group of men who met in the Colonial Tavern each day for lunch. About two times a year they would have a dinner, sometimes at Edgar Starbuck's camp. When the Colonial burned down in 1963, they began meeting at the Adelphi, but gradually a number of the members died and the group dissolved. Identification of the men in this photograph was done by Leo Roohan, Jr., standing on the right. They are: back row, John Nichols, county Republican chairman; Dutch Bigsby, Bigsby's Ford Dealership; Edgar Starbuck, president of Starbuck's Department Store; Dudley Lester, president Saratoga Vichy; L. W. Roohan, Sr., dentist; Fred Tarrant, president Tarrant Manufacturing; Frank Lawrence, insurance man and close friend of Settle; Harry B. Settle, photographer; "Ike" Burdick, insurance; Floyd Mason, telephone representative for New York Telephone; Bob Quinn, Colonial Tavern owner; Tom Luther, Luther Forest president—his father owned White Sulphur Springs; Frank Roohan, New York Telephone representative and a second cousin of L. W. Roohan, Leo Roohan, Jr. Second row: Jack Carey, president of Northern Distributing; W. J. Healey, Congress Gas and Oil; William H. Ford, Judge Ford's father. Front row: Phil J. Landry, dentist; T. J. Quilty, circulation manager of the Saratogian.

3047, H. B. Settle, Photographer, 1915

This Valentine party for children was held at the Todd home, 151 Nelson Avenue. Some of the children had rather elaborate costumes. The two young women in the first row wore dresses that were covered with hearts. The Todd family later moved to Circular Street and then to 4 Franklin Square to the house that is now known as the Marvin/Sackett/Todd house.

2776, H. B. Settle, Photographer, 1914
This was a corn husking bee. There is a possibility that the man reclining in front was H. B. Settle who took this photograph by depressing an air bulb that was connected by relay cord to the camera shutter.

10.096/3, H. B. Settle, Photographer, 1942
The black population of Saratoga Springs lived primarily on the west side of the city near an area originally called "Dublin" and then "Little Italy" after the waves of immigrants who had come to work on the railroad. Many blacks were employed by the hotels which were located close to the west side. Boardinghouses sprang up to accommodate some of the seasonal workers who preferred them to the accommodations offered by the hotels.

By the 1930s some businesses were owned by blacks and Congress Street was the center for all types of entertainment. This is a photograph of Jack's Harlem Club located at 56 Congress Street, with Isaiah Jackson, proprietor.

Most of the buildings in this area of Congress Street were demolished by Urban Renewal in the 1960s and 1970s.

7837/1, H. B. Settle, Photographer, 1934

The Wagon Wheel was a "speakeasy" located in Greenfield. By the time this photograph was taken, Prohibition had been repealed and Michael J. Sweeney was openly tending bar. The country was in the midst of the Depression in 1934, but entertainment spots in Saratoga remained popular. Another photograph of the Wagon Wheel showed Romeo Fenton and dancers entertaining the customers.

50-358/2, George S. Bolster, Photographer, 1950

Complete with drum majorettes and uniforms, the Cadet Corps Band was formed after World War II. It was the forerunner of the Avant Garde, a well-known drum corps that performed in Saratoga Springs until the mid 1980s. Fred Bolster, George's brother, was fourth from the right in the front row.

8372 detail, H. B. Settle, Photographer, 1936

This amusing photograph of the Spanish American War Veteran's Women's Auxiliary was taken in the United States Hotel Liberty Room on September 1, 1936. Over two thousand Spanish American War Veterans of the 38th National Encampment gathered in Saratoga Springs in September 1936 for memorial services, parades and business sessions.

76-53/1, Photographer unknown, 1976

In 1961 Duane LaFlesche, a Knickerbocker News editorialist from Albany, heard that the New York Philharmonic Orchestra had been invited to make its summer home in Stowe, Vermont. He wrote an editorial urging that the orchestra stay in New York State and that Saratoga be its summer home. At the same time Sen. Eustis Paine made a speech on the subject and Robert N. McKelvey, a Saratogian with the New York State Commerce Department, called Newman E. "Pete" Wait of the Adirondack Trust Company and Fred G. Eaton of the Saratogian.

New York State, under Gov. Nelson Rockefeller, was planning a three million dollar redevelopment of the Saratoga Spa and gave a twenty-five thousand dollar grant to study and draw up plans for a performing arts center. The three Saratogians, along with Charles Dake, president of Stewart's, began working.

The Martha Baird Rockefeller Foundation initially donated 1.2 million and other Rockefeller donations followed. Summer residents, led by Mrs. Ogden Phipps, contributed generously. Gene Robb, publisher of the Albany newspapers and Lewis Swyer, an Albany developer and supporter of the arts, joined in. Richard Leach was hired as SPAC director and convinced the Philadelphia Orchestra to make their summer home in Saratoga after the New York Philharmonic decided to go to Interlochen.

Five and one-half years later George Balanchine's New York City Ballet danced a Midsummer Night's Dream before a throng of construction workers, donors, campaign workers and their families. Today the Saratoga Performing Arts Center offers an array of entertainment each summer including the New York City Ballet, the New York City Opera, the Philadelphia Orchestra, and special popular programs. It has become a catalyst for the growth of the arts in the Capital Region.

7, Michael L. Noonan, Photographer, 1975

On Saturday October 4, 1975, Skidmore College and the Saratoga Arts Workshop presented their second annual Saratoga Folk Festival and Crafts Fair dedicated to Lena Spencer. In this photograph Lena Spencer; Kathy Radcliff (who later started and ran Lively Lucy's Coffeehouse at Skidmore); Jim Ringer, singer; Al McKenney and Rod Oleman, MC's of the event; and Mary McCaslin, lead guitar perform outside the Surrey Inn on the Skidmore campus.

For almost thirty years, Lena Spencer owned and operated Caffe Lena at 47 Phila Street in downtown Saratoga Springs. In May 1960 Lena Spencer, born Pasqualini Rosa Nargi in 1923, arrived in Saratoga Springs with her husband and founded the Caffe. Although she and her husband divorced a few years later, Lena remained to develop what was to become the longest continuously running coffee house in the United States. Folksingers including Bob Dylan, Arlo Guthrie, Maria Muldaur, Pete Seegar, Bruce "Utah" Phillips and many other famous names performed at the Caffe.

Living very simply, Lena managed to run the business on a shoestring and nurture and pay folksingers, actors and poets. Spencer made a small sixty-seat theater next to the Caffe available to playwrights and actors. In 1987 she received an honorary Doctor of Humane Letters from Skidmore College and in 1989 a Lifetime Achievement Award from the Saratoga County Arts Council. She died on October 23, 1989. The Caffe has continued to operate as a not-for-profit corporation since her death.

1093, H. B. Settle, Photographer, 1910

The Coon Club members held their hound and displayed twenty-one raccoon skins hanging on a board. On the right-hand side is the photographic pack of H. B. Settle. He is standing on the right-hand side of the front row in the picture using a hand-held bulb to trip the shutter for the picture.

2039/1, H. B. Settle, Photographer, 1913

Beside the Congress Spring Pavilion in Congress Park, groups of ice skaters and hockey players enjoyed a winter day. Winter sports were popular in Saratoga Springs and the Saratoga Winter Club was active in promoting both skating, tobogganing and snowshoeing.

In this photograph, portions of the Grand Union Hotel can be seen in the background. Congress Hall had been torn down, but the ballroom that is still on Spring Street can be seen through the open section of the Congress Spring Pavilion.

11.296/4, H. B. Settle, Photographer, 1946

Sen. Edgar T. Brackett bought nine hundred acres in Wilton in 1917 and had an eighteen-hole golf course constructed which he named McGregor for the nearby mountain. The McGregor Golf Links, a championship course, opened in 1920. Throughout the years the course has hosted many professional events. Homes have been built around the fairways and a swimming pool and tennis courts have been constructed.

72-75, Photographer unknown, circa 1900

The Saratoga Golf and Polo Club was established in 1896 by summer visitors who wanted to play golf, polo and tennis on grass courts during "the season" in Saratoga.

The original clubhouse, on the left in this photograph, was a modest building located on Church Street where the Adirondack Trust Company branch bank is today. In the early years, wealthy members would take turns paying any deficit incurred during the summer months.

By the 1968 there were more local members and the club purchased the Ostrander estate from "Paramount Pete" Issaris, who had run it as a restaurant called the Dorian. This estate abutted the original nine-hole course and the mansion became the clubhouse. Although polo is no longer played at the "Little Club," nine holes of golf, modern and grass tennis courts and a swimming pool are enjoyed by an active membership. The clubhouse remains a popular place for the parties of summer members.

81-08, Photographer unknown, circa 1930
Billiards and pool were played on Broadway above the present location of the Downstreet Marketplace. A group of rather serious spectators watched a match between Ruth McGinnis, who was apparently a professional woman player, and Bob Duval.

4905, H. B. Settle, Photographer, 1923
In his record book, H. B. Settle noted that he had photographed two baseball teams on the same day. They were probably playing each other in a league. The photograph of the Elks team deteriorated and was lost, but this photograph of the Company L team, with its very unusual mascot, survives in the collection.

74-101, J. S. Wooley, Photographer, circa 1910
The YMCA building on Broadway was a center for men's athletics in Saratoga Springs. It was obviously successful in its fundraising endeavors as the fifteen-thousand-dollar Club sign testified. The building contained storefronts on its lower level and a swimming pool and gymnasium. The Saratoga High School boys' swim team trained here as it was the only swimming facility in the village.

172

S-40, Photographer unknown, circa 1885

The 1895 Saratoga Springs Directory carried an advertisement for the "Casino Bicycle Academy." It was run by the Howland brothers and was located on Spring Street opposite Henry Street in an area that is now Congress Park but in 1895 was separate from the park. The ad exhorted people to examine the line of bicycles carried by Howland brothers before they purchased and said that lessons and instructions were given by professional teachers from New York City academies. "Have you taken your bicycle lessons for today? Bicycles taken care of by the day or week. For use of Academy with wheel, 15 cents. Bicycle Tandems for sale. Examine Spaulding's Leader for 1895. Bicycle Sundries for sale. Nothing but '95 bicycles in our livery. Up to date repairing done."

By 1900 the Bicycle Academy had become the Saratoga Furniture House with four thousand square feet of display space and by 1911 Richard Canfield had purchased the property, cleaned out the area and built the Italian Gardens behind Canfield Casino.

5733, H. B. Settle, Photographer, 1927

Members of the Jewish Athletic Club basketball team posed for their photograph. They were, left to right, front row: Milton Feller, Harry Schecter, Harry Feller, Ben Goldsmith and Lou Weinstein. Back row: Moe Schwartz, Leon Brown, Moe Fallick, Sam Covkin and Max Caplan.

55-368, George S. Bolster, Photographer and artist, 1955

George Bolster's son Fred was on the 1955 Van Raalte Little League team that won the National Division in Saratoga Springs. The teams that played in that division were listed in the upper right-hand corner. In the upper left-hand corner was the win/lost record. The win record was wiped out, but on the negative it said twenty-one.

George Bolster was well known for this type of artwork.

84-05, E. A. Record, Photographer, circa 1880

The Saratoga Winter Club had an elaborate and popular tobogganing area known as Glen Mitchell, which was located at the north end of Broadway. It received its name from the Glen Mitchell Hotel, which was operated in the area by Calib Mitchell and the Mitchell brothers. This hotel eventually became the original St. Clement's College. The property was next to the Henry Hilton Estate "Woodlawn Park" (the Skidmore College Campus today). Denton's Vly (a small lake) was also located in Woodlawn Park, and Hilton allowed it to be used for ice skating and ice boat racing.

On the back of the original photograph Thomas Carroll was identified as the builder of the slide. He was standing on the extreme right.

On the 1873 map of Saratoga Springs, Glen Mitchell was clearly marked. Just beyond it was a large area that was the Saratoga County Agricultural Fairgrounds and Racecourse.

81-03/4, Photographer unknown, circa 1865

In 1863 John Morrissey, a gambler who later built the Saratoga Club House (now the Casino in Congress Park), joined with William Travers, John Hunter and Leonard Jerome to form a racing association. Although the Civil War was in its third year and horses were difficult to find, a four-day racing program was held. The original track was in the Horse Haven area across the street from the present track. The first year was a great success and the Saratoga Racing Association purchased 125 acres across the road where they built the track and grandstand shown in this photograph.

AT SARATOGA RACE COURSE, JULY 31, 1893.

PAUL C. GRENING.   C. F. MASSEY,   R. P. FLOWER,   KING KAPURTHALA & WIFE,   GEN. B. F. TRACEY,   A. HIGGINS,
G. WALBAUM.   LIEUT. COL.   GOVERNOR,   AND SUITE OF INDIA.   SECRETARY OF THE NAVY.   U. S. SENATOR.
BRITISH ARMY.   STATE OF NEW YORK.   MRS. I. H. DAHLMAN.
MRS. G. WALBAUM.

79-65, Photographer unknown, 1893

Summers in Saratoga Springs became legendary, drawing dignitaries, politicians and the wealthy to partake of the pleasures of horse racing, gambling and the waters. In this 1893 photograph, P. P. Flower, governor of New York State, poses with a group at the Saratoga Racecourse.

By the following year criticism of gambling and racing had mounted. Gottfried Walbaum had purchased the track and was operating it in flagrantly dishonest ways, even providing a room where women and children could bet. The New York World sent crusading reporter Nelly Bly to write stories with captions like "The Shameful Story of Vice and Crime, Dissipation and Profligacy at This Once Most Respected Watering-Place." By the spring of 1896 only the Casino and five gambling establishments were given permission to open and the racetrack was purchased by a syndicate of wealthy sportsmen, headed by William C. Whitney, who immediately began restoring its prestige.

2169 detail, H. G. Ashby, Photographer, 1913

In June 1908 the Agnew-Hart Bill was passed in the New York State legislature. The governor of the state was Charles Evans Hughes, a crusader against gambling. This bill made it illegal to quote odds openly, solicit business or stand in a fixed place to record bets. Bookies at the track did all this and they, and their patrons, were arrested. In Saratoga some of the effects of the bill were not felt immediately because bookies began to take bets in their hotel rooms, but at the close of the 1910 racing season the track shut down. By 1913 a loophole was found in the law that permitted oral betting and the racetrack reopened, much to the joy of Saratoga citizens.

In this 1913 photograph patrons lined the rails as the horses lined up for the "old start." It was not until later that the starting gate was introduced.

55-52, Photographer unknown, circa 1900

Horse racing fans traveled to the track by carriages and by trolley. In this photograph both can be seen on East Avenue near the entrance to the racetrack.

176

3354/D, H. G. Ashby, Photographer, 1916

Willis Sharp Kilmer, in the long coat and sailor-straw hat and Walter M. Jeffords, Sr., watched the horses in the old paddock area at the racetrack. Kilmer owned a stable and was from a family that manufactured "Swamp Root" medicine. George Bolster, who was at one time a desk clerk at the Worden Hotel, overheard someone asking Kilmer what the medicine was good for. Kilmer answered, "a hundred years, I hope." The box for the medicine stated that: "'Swamp Root' tends to promote the flow of urine thereby aiding the kidneys in their necessary work of eliminating waste matter." The active ingredients were "extractives of Buchu Leaves, Cape Aloes and Peppermint Herb, Oil of Juniper, Venice Turpentine and Sucrose." There was a drawing of S. Andral Kilmer, M.D., on the bottle and a warning to diabetics. Another warning told about the small quantity of alcohol used to prevent fermentation. The alcohol content was 10 percent.

4233E, H. G. Ashby, Photographer, 1919
   Men in panama and sailor-straw hats, with a lone boy among them, lined the rail next to the old judge's stand. The distinctive Saratoga grandstand roofline can be seen clearly in the background. The name of the photographer, H. B. Ashby, is written on the bottom of some glass-plate negatives from 1913 to the 1940s. He was unknown to other photographers in Saratoga Springs and never signed the board for the press photographers that was in the H. B. Settle studio. His work was excellent and he had access to areas of the racetrack usually reserved for the press.

4233A, H. G. Ashby, Photographer, 1919
"Red Coat Murray" led the parade to the post at the Saratoga racetrack for over twenty-five years.

6006 detail, H. B. Settle, Photographer, 1928
A badly deteriorated negative in the George S. Bolster Collection revealed exercise boys relaxing and playing billiards in the "Jockey Y" which is located on the grounds of the Saratoga racetrack, across the street from the grandstand on Union Avenue. Doors are marked "Reading Room and Library" and "Correspondence Room."

6348/D, H. G. Ashby, Photographer, 1929

Watching the parade to the post, diners in the clubhouse were dressed in the latest 1920s fashions. The era of the Roaring Twenties ended in the Great Depression which began with the stock market crash of 1929. The 1930 summer season in Saratoga Springs continued as usual despite the hard-times in the rest of the country. However by the mid 1930s, society people had begun to tighten their belts and cut their social season to a bare minimum. The racetrack began to draw different clientele who came to gamble at the track and in the casinos and speakeasies which flourished both during Prohibition and after its repeal.

6348/E, H. G. Ashby, Photographer, 1929

At the Saratoga racetrack jockeys lined up to be weighed in on a scale that was set up under the trees. To this day jockeys are weighed in prior to each race. Extra weights are added to the saddle as deemed necessary by the handicapper. When the race is over, the jockey and saddle are weighed again to ensure that the proper weight was carried during the race.

9803/7, H. B. Settle, Photographer, 1941

Steeplechase racing has been part of the Saratoga racing program from the earliest days of the track. There are three tracks in the Saratoga oval: dirt, hurdle and turf, a mile grass course that was added in 1961. In this 1941 photograph, the horses cleared a water jump on the steeplechase course but because of his position, the fourth jockey looks headless.

9803/15, H. B. Settle, Photographer, 1941

The Agnew-Hart law which had pre-
vented bookies from openly soliciting bets on
horses at New York State tracks was
repealed in 1934. A hundred or more bookies
returned to Saratoga Springs, mounted the
betting stalls and commenced business. This
was only a brief interlude. Pari-mutuel
machines soon replaced them and an era of
colorful characters, chronicled by Damon
Runyon, disappeared from the track. Before
pari-mutuel betting, women had sent male
"runners" to place their bets. Now they
were permitted to line up at the windows
and place their own bets for the first time.

83-61/B, 1929, Michael L. Noonan, Photographer, entry card copied in 1983

The second year of racing in Saratoga Springs, 1864, saw the birth
of the Travers Stakes that were named in honor of William R.
Travers, president of the newly formed racing association. The race
was won by a colt called Kentucky, who was owned by Travers. The
Travers is the oldest stakes race for three-year-olds in the country
and second oldest on the North American continent. It was preceded
by the Queen's Plate in Ontario, Canada, which was first run in
1860. This official entry form from August 17, 1929, listed six races
on the ticket. The fifth was the Travers Stakes for three-year-olds. It
was won by Beacon Hill who was ridden by A. Robertson.

6350/B, H. G. Ashby, Photographer, 1929

The second week in August each year, yearling sales are held in the sales ring of the Fasig-Tipton Company. This was the original sales ring where prospective buyers, including the socially prominent racing families that congregate in Saratoga Springs each year, were seated while they or their agents could bid on unraced yearlings.

The sales were originally held in 1917 under the elms at the racetrack. In 1918 Samuel D. Riddle paid $5,000 for a colt he named Man O' War. "Big Red," as he was affectionately called, went on to win nearly $250,000 before he retired to stud. Ironically the only race that he lost was to Upset in the Stanford Stakes at Saratoga Springs.

A new sales ring, the Humphrey S. Finney Pavilion, was built in the late 1960s and named for the president of Fasig-Tipton. It is located on East Avenue two blocks north of the track.

Bloodlines, conformation and condition of the colts play an important part in the decision to bid. This is another form of gambling since most of the yearlings do not go on to become great winners.

72-108/8, Photographer unknown, circa 1900

A grandstand was erected on the polo field where well-dressed patrons could watch the matches in comfort. The 1900 Saratoga Directory lists the "Saratoga Polo Club, William H. Manning, treasurer: Office 1 Arcade: beyond Seward out limits." This is also where the field is today. Some of the original markers were found when the current field was being laid out.

72-108/9, Photographer unknown, 1901-1905

At the turn of the century, polo matches in Saratoga Springs were held under the auspices of the Saratoga Golf and Polo Club. Gradually the matches ceased to be held, and it was not until the past ten years that the sport was revived in this area.

Will Farrish and Peter Brant formed the Saratoga Polo Association and began bringing polo back to prominence. Advertisements state: "World Class High Goal Polo. Join us for an exciting season featuring the top players from Argentina, France, England and the United States."

Each of the eight players in the match has at least six polo ponies to ride during the six chukkers of the game. The skill and daring of the riders make this an exciting spectator sport. In recent years, Skidmore College has been sponsoring both men's and women's polo teams that are competing on an intercollegiate level.

55-364, George S. Bolster, Photographer, 1955

In 1950 the idea of collecting and preserving "all materials and articles associated with the origin, history and development of horse racing and the breeding of the thoroughbred horse" resulted in the founding of the National Musuem of Racing, which was chartered by the Regents of the state of New York at that time.

Cornelius Vanderbilt Whitney was the first president and George D. Widener and newspaperman Nelson Dunson were the principal founders. The Grand Union Hotel was looked at as a possible site, but the price of that building became prohibitive. For four years the exhibits were displayed by the Historical Society of Saratoga Springs in a ground floor room in Canfield Casino (now the Ann Grey Gallery and gift shop).

When the New York Racing Association was formed, private stockholders in the old racing association sold their stock and, according to Elaine Mann, former director of the Racing Museum, "these wonderful gentlemen took that money and bought a lot across from the racetrack in order to erect the museum." She also recalled that the Chamber of Commerce put on a fund drive to raise money locally.

In this photograph the cornerstone is being put in place. Left to right, are: George Wertime, the contractor, Walter M. Jeffords, Sr., who became the second president of the Board of Trustees, F. Skiddy von Stade and Bayard Tuckerman, Jr.

By 1957 an addition was added called "Patrons of the Turf" which housed three galleries showing famous people instrumental in keeping racing alive. In 1960 Walter M. Jeffords, Sr., opened an additional wing. When he died in October of the same year the wing became the Walter M. Jeffords Memorial Wing.

71488/15, Michael L. Noonan, Photographer, 1988

At the end of the 1987 racing season, the National Museum of Racing closed for a total, year-long renovation. The renovation was suggested by Paul Mellon who thought that, although the museum was beautiful, it had become "static." Exciting renovations had taken place at museums in Haymarket, England, and at the Kentucky Derby Museum in Louisville. Specialists Ivor Heal Design Company and Tempus Exhibition and Museum Consultants from England were hired. A fund drive was spearheaded by Paul Mellon and Whitney Tower.

Visitors now enter the museum through a starting gate complete with sounds of horses loading, jockeys yelling and stalls flying open. The focus of the museum has changed from collection and display to education. In this photograph, visitors to the museum are shown listening to jockeys and trainers in a re-creation of the paddock area.

75-51 detail, Photographer unknown, 1947

On June 26, 1941, the Saratoga Raceway opened as the first pari-mutuel track to be designed and built for racing under the lights. W. Ellis Gilmour pioneered the idea. He was joined by Frank L. Wiswall, an Albany attorney who was secretary of the New York State Harness Racing Commission, Elbridge T. Gerry, first chairman of the commission and Dunbar W. Bostwick, a wealthy Vermont industrialist.

The track was built on the former Whitney estate which was owned by Willard J. Grande. After a few years of successful operation, World War II intervened. The track closed from 1943 to 1945. Then Frank Wiswald became president and served for eighteen years to be succeeded by Ernest B. Morris in 1963. Morris was the former district attorney of Albany County and a racing commissioner. Morris expanded and modernized the facility and popularized

harness racing both locally and nationally. Attendance at the Raceway reached a peak in the late sixties and early seventies with 650,000 patrons in a year.

Ernest Morris was succeeded by his son David, a lawyer, in 1978. Saratoga's track remained relatively popular, although harness racing across the nation was experiencing a decline in attendance and many tracks were closing. In 1987 Upstate Harness Racing, Incorporated, purchased the track and is the current owner and operator.

In this 1947 photograph the following are identified as: lead horse ridden by Jack Wiswall; No. 1 horse (Syndicator) driven by Garland Garnsey; No. 2, unidentified; No. 3, driver Dick Webber; No. 4, unidentified; No. 5, driver Del Cameron; No. 6, driver Henry Thomas; No. 7, driver Billy Haughton and No. 8, unidentified.

2914, H. B. Settle, Photographer, 1915
    The original Adirondack Trust Company Building occupied the same site as the current building at the southwest corner of Broadway and Church Street. It was a modest building surrounded by businesses on each side selling tires. Notice the cut down Packard in front of John Hutchin's tire store on Church Street.
    Advertisements in the 1915 Saratoga Directory stated that the company "Issues special deposit books for any amount bearing interest at 4 percent" and "Summer cottagers will be pleased with our arrangements. We solicit their accounts."

Cornerstone
For A Community

A D I R O N D A C K
T R U S T   C O M P A N Y

On June 10, 1916, while European armies slaughtered one another in what became known as the Great War, a group of Americans — businessmen, politicians, workers and just the plain curious — gathered at the corner of Church Street and Broadway in Saratoga Springs. The occasion: records, papers and other items were being placed in the cornerstore of the Adirondack Trust Company building, a new bank being built for a financial institution that was fifteen years old at the time.

The Adirondack Trust Company had begun with a meeting of village leaders on May 8, 1901. Among those who were included on the bank's "notice of intention to organize" were James Mingay, Charles Bullock, William Worden and Douglass Mabee. On September 21 of that year the first meeting of the bank's board of directors was held at the Broadway office of James L. Scott, one of the founders. Worden was made chairman, and at a subsequent meeting held at his Worden Hotel on October 5, Edgar T. Brackett was elected to the board of directors and made president of the bank. Mingay was named first vice president, Bullock second vice president and Mabee third vice president. Scott was made secretary and Frank Howland treasurer. One item of business completed at this meeting was a report that the bank had taken a lease with the owners of the Wescott Building at the southwest corner of Broadway and Church Street with the intention of renting the corner store. Into this new bank was installed a thirty-three-ton vault. It was so large that the Church Street wall of the original building had to be torn out to get it in.

Later, when the present building was constructed, the huge vault was left in place and the newer structure was built around it.

One of those involved in the bank's early years and the main force behind the construction of the building was New York State Senator Edgar T. Brackett, well known at the Spa for leading the efforts to stop gas companies from destroying the town's springs by siphoning off carbonic acid gas for use in such items as ice cream sodas, a popular treat in the Victorian era. Brackett, forty days shy of his sixty-third birthday when the bank's cornerstone was sealed, was in his fourteenth year as president of Adirondack Trust in 1916, and his signature appears on a letter placed in the cornerstone. The letter, addressed to whomever should be serving as directors of the bank when it is razed, ended with a paragraph that expressed a hope for peace in future generations: "This letter is written in the time of the great war ravaging more than one-half the civilized world. We express to you our earnest hope that it is the last great conflict in which the world shall engage; that out of it shall come conditions that shall forbid all wars and make for universal and enduring peace; that because of it shall be discovered means other than the sword by which nations may settle their grievances and that most of all, the opening of this letter shall find the great Republic still young and fresh in its ideals of liberty and equality, the leader and dominant figure of the world."

Other items, along with Brackett's letter, remain in the cornerstone, including a copy of the company charter, copies of daily papers from June 9, 1916; coins from the era, a copy of the bank's first statement, showing deposits of $113,000 and the latest statement of 1916 showing deposits of more than $3,000,000. Richard Mingay, a brother of James Mingay, one of Adirondack Trust's founders, donated a copy of the village charter from 1857, a copy of the *Daily Saratogian* dated July 6, 1876, and a collection of coins dating back to the Civil War.

Less than six months after the cornerstone was sealed, the bank opened its doors on New Year's Day, 1917, to give the citizens of Saratoga Springs an advance look at the building that would become a community and architectural landmark that has outlasted many of its contemporaries. One day after

the open house, Adirondack Trust accepted its first deposit in its new building. The date was January 2, 1917, fifteen years after the bank first opened at the same site, doing business on the first floor of a building that also was home to tire and piano shops.

When demolition of the old building at the corner of Church and Broadway began on March 6, 1916, Adirondack Trust moved to temporary headquarters across the street and remained there until moving into the newly completed building on December 31, 1916, after a little more than nine months of construction. What Saratogians saw on that cold first day of 1917 is much the same as it is today. "The danger of overdecoration has been scrupulously avoided," said an article in the Saratogian of December 30, 1916. "Simplicity is the note at which the creators of the building aimed, and the beauty of simplicity is apparent in its exterior and interior."

The building's exterior is made of white Vermont marble. Two Grecian columns give an imposing yet open quality to the bank's entrance, where the main doors, made of bronze and weighing several tons, are decorated with an Adirondack scene in which stags, the company's symbol of strength and stability, graze in a mountain setting. Other stags' heads decorate the massive chandeliers that hang from the bank's forty-five-foot ceilings. Another stag's head appears on the ornament that crowns the main facade, which also features horns of plenty and American eagles, "always a patriotic and effective architectural ornament," noted Alfred Hopkins, the New York City architect who designed the building. George B. Wills and Company, another New York City firm, was hired to build the bank.

Adorning the four walls inside the bank are proverbs researched by Brackett:

"Saving is a greater art than earning. A penny saved is a pound earned."

"Diligence is the parent of Fortune."

"The first years of a man must make provision for the last."

"Frugality is the mother of the virtues."

That Brackett tried his hand at copywriting is no surprise. He coined Adirondack Trust's motto — "It Has the Strength of the Adirondacks" — and even wrote the bank's advertisements that appeared in the *Saratogian* four times a week during the 1910s. A

5690/1, Photographer unknown, 1903
The original employees of the Adirondack Trust Company who were in this photograph were, left to right: J. P. Wemple, general banker; Waldo Rich, teller; William B. White, banker; A. W. Shepherd, Jr., banker; Wesley Allen, janitor and F. G. Howland, treasurer.

78-20, Photographer unknown, 1902
The vault for the Adirondack Trust Company was moved into place. The new bank building was built around it in 1916. In the photograph the workmen were moving the door of the vault down from the D.&H. Railroad Station on Railroad Place. The man in front, although unidentified, was probably from the Mosler Safe Company.

veteran of several political campaigns, he knew the value of getting a person's attention with newspaper advertisements featuring large, bold-faced type and forceful statements, even if they bordered on the corny. Under the made-up headline of "Made Mattress Her Bank," he warned against the practice of keeping money under one's bed by relating the supposedly true story of a woman who threw out her mattress and the eighteen hundred dollars she had hidden there.

Adirondack Trust was competing for depositors with two other banks in town, so Brackett's effusive prose could be seen as good old American one-up-manship. Said one ad: "They Say That A Boy Killing Snakes Is The Busiest Thing In Nature. For The Next Busiest See Our Office During Rush Hour."

Brackett's advertisements rarely were adorned with illustrations. Words were inexpensive and to the point. An Adirondack Trust advertisement that ran in the *Saratogian* on July 22, 1915, featured the words WARSAW THREATENED at the top, while underneath it read, "From The Military Standpoint But We Are IMPREGNABLE." Once the United States had entered the war in 1917, Brackett played on the patriotic fervor gripping the nation with an ad in April 1918 that admonished OLD TIGHT WAD for not giving money to help out the war effort being fought by "The Boys On The Battle Line." Then, in a stretch of the imagination not uncommon for Brackett, he penned: "Saving Is Going To Win The War."

The man who liked to write advertising copy for his bank was a Saratoga County native raised in Iowa, far from the Adirondack Mountains he viewed as a metaphor for trust and solid reputation. Edgar Truman Brackett was born in the town of Wilton, just north of Saratoga Springs, on July 30, 1853. His father built railroad bridges, his mother liked to read, especially Edgar Allen Poe, whom she named her son after. While still a child the Bracketts moved halfway across the still-young nation to Mount Vernon, Iowa. After graduating from Cornell College in Mount Vernon, he returned to Saratoga Springs, where his grandfather lived, and began to study law with the firm of Pond and French. He was admitted to the bar in 1875, and the following year Pond and French became Pond, French and Brackett. He later ran his

own practice from 1892 until 1917, when the firm of Brackett, Todd, Wheat and Wait was organized.

Brackett, a staunch Republican, entered politics in the 1890s and was elected to the New York State Senate in 1895. He served in the Senate from 1896 to 1906 and from 1908 until 1912. Considered a man of extraordinary charm and integrity, Brackett was also known for being straightforward when it came to his politics. When he died, the New York Tribune wrote of him: "Had Senator Brackett been a trifle less outspoken in his opinions, a little more compromising in his views, he might easily have become Governor or United States Senator, but to him his political fortunes were of far less importance than perfect freedom to speak his mind even though this pleasure sometimes multiplied his enemies."

His biggest enemies were the insurance companies. Early on in his career in state politics Brackett introduced reform bills aimed at ending the insurance industry's dominance over New York politicians. He constantly called for investigations into the life insurance companies in the state, and after eight years of Brackett's urging, those investigations took place. When the opposition party sought to remove a bootblack Brackett had installed in the Capitol, every page boy in the state legislature had his shoes shined every day by Brackett's man — with Brackett picking up the cost. "They are the most willing lot of boys I ever saw," the senator from Saratoga County said, "I am willing to pay and they are willing to let me."

Brackett's charity to others was well known in Saratoga. While he was diligent in his responsibilities of overseeing other people's money, Brackett nevertheless was not the frugal man his mottoes would lead one to believe. Skidmore College, the hospital, churches, homes for orphans, widows, the infirm — all at one time or another benefited from Brackett being an "easy mark." Some took advantage of his unbridled charity. After his death in 1924, a memoriam book said of Brackett: "He gave on with hands torn by the fangs he had tried to feed."

Besides the Adirondack Trust building, Brackett was behind the construction of a theater in Saratoga Springs and McGregor Links Country Club in his birthplace of Wilton. His efforts to save the springs were enough to endear him to Saratogians for generations. When he died in February 1924 at the age of

LAYING CORNER STONE, ADIRONDACK TRUST CO,
JUNE 10-1916

11690/2, Thomas Magovern, Photographer, 1916

On June 10, 1916, the cornerstone ceremony for the new Adirondack Trust Company was held. The man reading the proclamation was Sen. Edgar T. Brackett, president of the Adirondack Trust Company. Beside him on the left of the photograph was Frank Howland, treasurer and secretary. At the center on the right was Douglass W. Mabee. Other officers of the company in 1916 were

Charles C. Bullock and Charles Van Deusen, vice president. Current directors of the Adirondack Trust Company are: Vassar H. Curtis; Alfred J. Farone, Jr.; Willard E. Grande; Thomas J. Healy; Kent E. Jones; Douglass M. Mabee; David H. Porter; Robert E. Rockwell; Leo W. Roohan, Jr.; Harry D. Snyder; Stanley L. VanRensselaer; Charles V. Wait and Jane A. Wait.

seventy, his funeral procession passed beneath the gateway at the entrance to Congress Park, whose springs he helped rescue from the gas companies. Townspeople had the gateway erected as a show of gratitude for what the senator had done, and Brackett, as one of his final wishes, was borne through the park to his final resting place in Greenridge Cemetery.

Some last names of bank officers that appear early in Adirondack Trust's history still remain a part of the institution. Newman E. Wait served as bank president from 1934 until 1961, after which his son, Newman E. "Pete" Wait, assumed the president's position until his death in 1983. And Charles V. Wait, son of Pete and grandson of Newman, became president in 1984

and still serves. Mabees have been involved with Adirondack Trust since its inception. Douglass W. Mabee was a founder of Adirondack Trust and his son, also named Douglass W., served with the father on the bank's board of directors for many years. Douglass W. Mabee II served on the board of directors for thirty-five years, from 1947 until 1982, and his son, Douglass M. "Tim" Mabee, continues the family tradition by also serving as a director. And the Brackett name, so important to Adirondack Trust's history, could still be found on the bank's roll call of directors as recently as the late 1980s, when Elizabeth Brackett Moore, the senator's granddaughter, resigned her directorship.

78-42/2, Photographer unknown, circa 1910
Sen. Edgar T. Brackett, front left, was photographed with two other unidentified gentlemen. The badge with a ribbon that the gentlemen in the back is wearing on his lapel was a Saratoga County Republican badge issued by Senator Brackett.

Through its nine decades, the Adirondack Trust Company has seen the neighborhood go through several changes, from the bustling, hotel-lined high-life of the early 1900s through the faded resort image of the 1950s and early 1960s. Since then the city can boast of several new hotels — including the Holiday Inn, which bought the building that had previously been the first-ever community-owned hotel in the nation and was backed by the Adirondack Trust. The new Skidmore College campus, the Saratoga Performing Arts Center and the Saratoga Springs City Center were projects which had a Wait behind them — Newman, Pete and Charles, respectively. Through all of Saratoga's changes, Adirondack Trust has re-mained what it started out to be, a community bank. When a national business magazine named Adirondack Trust one of the hundred safest banks in America, the switchboard at the Broadway bank was flooded with hundreds of calls each day from people as far away as Hawaii and Alaska wanting to put their money into Adirondack Trust's certificates of deposit. But the bank turned down the offers. It was not interested in money that would be here today and gone the next. Adirondack Trust's directors wanted to keep the focus of their bank on Saratoga Springs and its surrounding communities. Edward Truman Brackett would have strongly seconded that motion.

11690/8, Winn Hill, Photographer, 1950
 People waited in line to do business at the Adirondack Trust Company in this 1950
photograph. Today the tellers' windows are not located in the middle section of the building,
but are along the north and south walls.

72890/17, Michael L. Noonan, Photographer, 1990
Built over a nine month period ending July 17, 1990, the newest branch office of the
Adirondack Trust Company evokes the proud traditions of the past in a post-modern style.

Unnumbered, Randall Perry, Photographer, 1989

The officers and staff of the main office of the Adirondack Trust Company posed for this 1989 Christmas photograph. They are left to right, row one: Charles Wait, William Colonell, Richard Ferguson, Timothy Schlachter, Margaret Roohan, Kathleen McDonough and Karen Moak-Stutz. Row two: Sharon VanWinkler, Elena Lupino, Gregory DiMartino, Roxanne Relyea, Tracy Lynch, Constance Foley, Lillian Traynor, Sharon Rivers, Jill Henning, Gail Pastor, Carol Catone and Barbara Ryan. Row three: Helen Bryant, Jan Waring, Heidi Kunath, Caroline Putman, Janis Burgess, John Boyd, John Jordan, Pamela Barrington, Dana Parry, Greta Clements, Donna Derby, Tammy Wolfe and Jeannine Moore. Row four: Michael Costanza, John Eagleson, Bruce Grundy, Meredith Covell, Dena Cogan, Shannon Tuttle, Richard Carman, Clark Curtis, David Brown, Stacey Richmond, Eleanor Ryan, Donnamarie Ferro, Christine Perry, June Ray and Bridget Jennings. Row five: Lisa Walbridge, Michael Meslar, Sharon Maas, Rita Armitage, Cathy Taylor, Carole Murtha, Debra Peterson, Lorraine D'Amato, Vassar Curtis, Gretchen Guckemus, Susan Welch, Kelley Hathaway, Graydine Sanders, Marianne McCarthy and Jenifer Riggi. Row six: Elizabeth Bowen, Megan Marr, Julie Brasser, Brenda Rourke and Jason Robinson. Missing: Tammy Bethel, Dawn Brown, Selma Clark, James Conners, Darlene Coon, Virginia Corey, Ruth Ann Danaher, Shirley Galligan, Whitney Hunt, Gay Izzo, Mary Kellerhouse, Edward King, Betty Kirkpatrick, Denise Lake, Kimberly Lennox, Charlene Leslie, Geraldine Mann, Freda Martino, Darlene Meader, Richard Miglucci, Christine Muller, Angeline O'Rourke, Judy Pierce, John Priest, Henry Priester, Ruth Purtell, Michele Richardson, Margaret Schulz, Karen Stetkar, Christina Toleman, Martina Vicha, Jeanette Wall, Valerie Willette, Susan Willett and Gail Wilson.

197

Adirondack Trust Company charter, 8 May, 1901.

Adirondack Trust Company, minutes of meeting of Board of Directors, 21 September 1901.

Adirondack Trust Company, minutes of meeting of Board of Directors, 5 October 1901.

Adirondack Trust Company, minutes of meeting of Board of Directors, 31 October 1901.

Adirondack Trust Company, minutes of meeting of Board of Directors, 2 January 1902.

_____. "The Adirondack Trust Company: How We Built It." Saratoga Springs, N.Y.: *The Saratogian*, 1916.

_____. "In Memoriam: Edgar Truman Brackett." Albany, N.Y. J. B. Lyon Company, 1924.

_____. "Public Invited To New Trust Company Building Monday." *The Saratogian*, 30 December 1916.

_____. "Brackett's Unusual Ads Asking for Accounts Put Adirondack Trust Co. on Firm Footing." *The Saratogian*, 26 October 1954.

_____. "Writes Letter To Be Read In 2016." *The Saratogian*, 10 June 1916.

Armstead, Myra Beth Young. "History of Blacks in Resort Towns: Newport, Rhode Island and Saratoga Springs, New York, 1870-1930." Ph.D. diss., University of Chicago, March 1987.

Dunn, Violet B., Robert S. Hayden and Clayton H. Brown. "Saratoga County History." Syracuse, N.Y.: Salina Press Inc., 1974.

Doctorow, E. L. *Billy Bathgate*. New York: Random House, 1989.

Gilbert, Jersey and Elizabeth M. MacDonald. "The 100 Safest Banks." *Money*, October 1989.

History of The Delaware and Hudson Company. Albany: J. B. Lyon Company, 1925.

Jensen, Oliver. "Windows On Another Time." *American Heritage*, March 1988.

Kirk, Margaret O. "Picture This." *USAir Magazine*, June 1989.

McGregor, Jean. *Chronicles of Saratoga*. Series of articles reprinted from *The Saratogian*. Saratoga Springs, N.Y.: Bradshaw Printing Co., 1947.

Newhall, Beaumont. *The History of Photography*. Boston: Little, Brown, and Company, 1982.

Rosenblum, Naomi. *A World History of Photography*. New York: Abbeville Press, 1984.

Saratogian, The Editorial. "James A. Leary, man of power." 25 October 1963.

Shaughnessy, Jim. *Delaware & Hudson*. Berkeley, Calif.: Howell-North Books, 1967.

Sparkle, Sophie. *Sparkles From Saratoga*. New York: American News Co., 1881.

Smith, Richard Norton. *Thomas E. Dewey and His Times*. New York: Simon and Schuster, 1982.

Stoddard, Seneca Ray. *Saratoga and Lake George*. Albany: Van Benthuysen & Sons, 1881.

Stonequist, Martha. "1890 Saratoga invention still helps hurt stop hurting." *The Saratogian*, 12 July 1989

_____. "Hawley name brings back memories." *The Saratogian*, 8 November 1989.

Swanner, Grace Maguire, M.D. *Saratoga: Queen of Spas*. Utica, N.Y.: North Country Books, Inc., 1988.

Sweeney, Bea. "Worden Hotel filled with memories." *The Saratogian*, 23 May 1985.

_____. "Hotel Revamped after Civil War." *The Saratogian*, 30 May 1985.

_____. "Saratoga Prints at Worden Hotel." *The Saratogian*, 6 June 1985.

_____. "Worden Hotel leading hostelry." *The Saratogian*, 13 June 1985.

_____. "Congress Hall another of Saratoga's famous hotels." *The Saratogian*, 13 February 1986.

_____. "Congress Hall was fashionable among elite visitors." *The Saratogian*, 20 February 1986.

_____. "Saratoga Springs Community works to improve image." *The Saratogian*, 27 February 1986.

_____. "Citizens plan to rebuild hotel after disasterous fire." *The Saratogian*, 6 March 1986.

_____. "Susan B. Anthony visits Congress Hall." *The Saratogian*, 13 March 1986.

_____. "The demise of the Congress Hall." *The Saratogian*, 20 March 1986.

Sullivan, Frank. "'They're Off' at Saratoga!" *New York Times*, 2 August 1970.

Waller, George. *Saratoga: Saga of an Impious Era*. Prentice-Hall, 1966.

INDEX TO PHOTOGRAPHERS AND PHOTOGRAPHS

All photographs for this book were printed by Michael L. Noonan from original negatives where possible, on Kodabromide archival fiber based paper. Photographer, negative number, subject, size of the negative (in inches), type of negative and the page number are listed.

55-368	Little League	4x5 safety film	174
55-364	Racing Museum	4x5 safety film	186

Also, front and back cover photographs were hand-colored in transparent oil color by George Bolster.

BROWN, H. G.

70-119/2	Citizen's Corps	4x5 copy negative	132

COOK, C. C.

72-67/1	Steeplechase	4x5 copy negative	18

D'ARRIGO, Heisler

77-42	Dewey	4x5 copy negative	36

DOUBLEDAY and KNIGHT

2522	Harrison	8x10 glass plate copy neg by H. B. Settle in 1913	48

DURKEE COLLECTION

73-82	Civil War	4x5 copy negative	131

EPLER and ARNOLD

73-15	Madame Carlotta	4x5 copy negative	back cover

EPLER, Harrison J.

65-150/16	Regatta	4x5 copy negative	148

GURTLER, J. B.

77-45/105	Lorey	5x7 cellulose nitrate	19

HILL, Winn

11690/8	ATC	4x5 copy negative	195

HILTON, Albert B.

62-277/8	Hilton	4x5 copy negative	78
62/227/4	Hilton	4x5 copy negative	78

HUTCHINS, Charles H.

unnumbered	Conv. Hall	4x5 safety film	33
63/96/3	N.Y. Tel.	4x5 safety film	38
50/331/3	Tiger Club	4x5 safety film	166

LOREY, Gustave

70-115	Saratoga Nat. Bank	4x5 copy negative	105
74-82	Saratoga High 1923	4x5 copy negative	110

MAGOVERN, Thomas F.

81-02	Bench and Bar	4x5 copy negative	38
11.667	SHS football team	4x5 copy negative	111
72-204/1	Grade school band	4x5 copy negative	12
11690/2	ATC cornerstone	4x5 copy negative	193

MYERS, Hank
82-12	Skidmore Theater	4x5 copy negative	117

NOONAN, Kristin D.
22090	Noonan portrait	4x5 safety film	208

NOONAN, Michael L.
122987	ATC winter morning	4x5 safety film	9
86-27	Photographers sign-in	4x5 safety film	23
85-44/8	Bolster handcoloring	2 1/4x2 3/4 safety	23
84-41/16	S.S. City Center	2 1/4x2 3/4 safety	34
81-44	Grand Union site	4x5 safety film	58
11889	Sullivan/Magovern letter	4x5 copy negative	70
71388	Yaddo fellows	2 1/4x2 3/4 safety	122
85-68/3	Four Winds Hospital	2 1/4x2 3/4 safety	130
87-31/6	HSSS Belter exhibit	2 1/4x2 3/4 safety	142
7	Lena Spencer folk fest.	2 1/4x2 3/4 safety	170
83-61/B	Travers card 1929	4x5 copy negative	184
71488/15	Museum of racing	2 1/4x2 3/4 safety	187
72890/17	ATC So. Broadway branch	2 1/4x2 3/4 safety	196
21690	Mastrianni	2 1/4x2 3/4 safety	208
12290	Carola	2 1/4x2 3/4 safety	208

also 4x5 Ektachrome transparencies of the front and back cover photographs were taken by Michael Noonan.

PERRY, Randall
unnumbered	ATC and employees	4x5 copy negative	197

RECORD and EPLER
74-46	Blizzard '88	4x5 copy negative	8 & 59
78-21/12	Presby., general assembly	4x5 copy negative	87

RECORD, E. A.
70-133/12	Firesled	4x5 copy negative	24
84-05	Glen Mitchell Toboggan	4x5 copy negative	174

SCHNEIDER, Ralph
unnumbered	Hutchins/Settle	4x5 cellulose nit.	22

SETTLE, Harry B.
3229	Hathorn No. 3 Spring	8x10 glass plate	16
8878/1detail	Broadway-Tom Magovern	8x10 cellulose nit.	20
1	Union Wheel Club	5x7 glass plate	22
1420	Post Office ext.	8x10 glass plate	28
10-711	War Bond parade	4x5 safety film	30
6676	Fire House-Lake Ave.	8x10 cellulose nit.	32
8352	Ad. Mallery/Hopi Ind.	8x10 cellulose nit.	37
3730	City Council-New Chart.	8x10 glass plate	40
9574	Drs. Leonard/Ressigue	4x5 safety film	40
6556	Leary/Fullerton	8x10 cell. nit copy negative (1929)	41
5838/5	Adirondack Depot	8x10 cell. nitrate	47
9779/1	Drink Hall interior	8x10 safety film	49

63	Chapman family	8x10 glass plate	50
599/1	Mayor Pettee/bear	8x10 glass plate	51
6359	"Pitney's" airport	8x10 cell. nitrate	52
7384	Grand Union Crystal Rm.	8x10 cell. nitrate	53
8076	Ross-Ketchum	8x10 cell. nitrate	54
8342	Bill Ford's Esso	8x10 cell. nitrate	54
72-60B	Broadway aerial	5x7 cell. nitrate	55
113	Nat. Eclectic Med. Asscn.	11x14 glass plate	56
52-260	Grand Union lobby	4x5 safety	58
9305/4	U.S. Hotel bar	4x5 safety	62
8480/1	Gangsters	10x15 cm. cell. nit.	62
1537/3	Broadway/W. Circular	8x10 glass plate	64
4322	Columbian Hotel	8x10 cell. nitrate	64
4787A	Saratoga Inn	5x7 glass plate	67
9809	Gideon Putnam Hotel	8x10 safety film	67
7615/7	The Brook	8x10 cell. nitrate	68
7491/2	Grand Union Hotel	5x7 glass plate	72-73
3511/D	McCormack/Olcott	5x7 glass plate	76
6013	Grippin Groceries	8x10 cell. nitrate	76
2977	Grippin family	8x10 glass plate	77
2139	Wallbridge family	8x10 glass plate	80
5929	Dr. Grant/Elks Club	8x10 cell. nitrate	82
7351/2	Elks Club tour	8x10 cell. nitrate	82
1309detail	Andrews attic	8x10 glass plate	83
10.632/1	D.A.R./Walworth	4x5 safety film	83
79A	Gage-Ellis wedding	8x10 glass plate	84
5637	Todd family	8x10 cell. nitrate	85
6370	Todd house interior	8x10 cell. nitrate	86
2576	Schwarte family	8x10 glass plate	86
9701	Presbyterian Ch. ext.	8x10 cell. nitrate	88
159	Methodist Ch. ext.	11x14 glass plate	88
9365	Methodist Ch. choir	5x7 cell. nitrate	90
11.247	St. Peter's pageant	4x5 safety film	92
52.18/1	Bethesda Epis. int.	4x5 safety film	92
4355	Hall's Oyster House	8x10 cell. nitrate	95
5734	Saraspa Manors	8x10 cell. nitrate	96
151A	Collamer building	11x14 glass plate	98-99
6083detail	Caroline Street	8x10 cell. nitrate	100
7336/2	Paramount int.	8x10 cell. nitrate	101
6539	Thomas Lunch Room	8x10 cell. nitrate	101
6642/B	Simon's/Columbian Hotel	8x10 cell. nitrate	102
7303	Hewitt/Woolworth/Star.	8x10 cell. nitrate	103
5574	Starbuck/employees	8x10 cell. nitrate	103
10-369/1detail	Goldsmith	4x5 safety film	106
2003	Tarrant Mfg group	8x10 glass plate	106
6627	1910 class reunion	8x10 cell. nitrate	109
9982	School No. 3/Mrs. Hall	4x5 safety film	111
51-165	SHS grads.	5x7 safety film	113
12.092	St. Clement's 8th grade	4x5 safety film	113
9415	SPA H. S. grads.	8x10 safety film	114
6255	Eastman School of Bus.	8x10 cell. nitrate	114
2773	St. Faiths School	8x10 glass plate	115
2029	Lucy Scribner/Miss Smith	8x10 glass plate	116
1095	Mrs. Weeks sewing group	8x10 glass plate	117
1572	1st Skid. grad. class	8x10 glass plate	118
2528	Skidmore art class	8x10 glass plate	118
2597/4	Skidmore tennis team	8x10 glass plate	119

7479/9	Skidmore grad class	4x6 glass plate	120
4201/1	House of Panza	5x7 glass plate	123
11.330	Orig. Saratoga Hospital	4x5 safety film	126
6272	Saratoga Hosp. nurses	8x10 cell. nitrate	127
5757	Sara. Hospital lab	8x10 cell. nitrate	127
12.573	Harvey Mfg. Co.	8x10 safety film	128
3461/1	Dr. Moriarta Emanator.	8x10 glass plate	129
1814	Sara. Monument dedic.	5x7 glass plate	133
3530/2	Co. L. boarding train	5x7 glass plate	134
9555/6	Bundles for Brit.	4x6 safety film	135
10.711/2	SHS War Bond parade	4x5 safety film	135
10.269	Gurtler Bros Post 420	4x5 safety film	136
10.252	Skidmore Air Wardens	4x5 safety film	136
D71-28	World's Fount. of Youth	4x6 cell. nitrate	138
1632detail	Hillside bandstand	8x10 glass plate	140
3742	Casino exterior	8x10 glass plate	140
126	Casino dining room	8x10 glass plate	141
1328	Casino gaming room	8x10 glass plate	141
3317/2	Italian gardens	8x10 glass plate	141
3216	Trask Memorial	8x10 glass plate	142
4790/A	Bandstand/Casino	5x7 glass plate	142
4766A	Trask stairway	5x7 glass plate	143
4239/3	Water slide/Kaydeross	5x7 glass plate	144
2973/1	Ice-Saratoga Lake	8x10 glass plate	144
5605/3	Dempsey/White Sul. Spr.	8x10 cell. nitrate	145
9437	Riley's staff	8x10 safety film	146
9882/2	N.Y. Tel./Newman's	4x5 safety film	149
6090/3	Elks/Arrowhead	8x10 cell. nitrate	149
3225	High Rock Bath House	8x10 glass plate	151
3223	Emperor Spg.	8x10 glass plate	152
3189	Hathorn No. 1 interior	8x10 glass plate	153
8713	Hathorn fire	10x15 cm. cell. nit.	154
222/2	Patterson Spg. int.	8x10 glass plate	155
4239/7	Washington Bath House	5x7 glass plate	156
8728	Mud baths	10x15 cm. cell. nit.	157
8662	Lincoln Baths ext.	8x10 cell. nitrate	157
3222	Breakfast-Geyser	8x10 glass plate	158
6165detail	Hayes Well	8x10 cell. nitrate	158
549	Carbonic Gas tanks	8x10 glass plate	159
8483A	Sara. Vichy Plant int.	10x15 cm. cell. nit.	159
7480/2	Hall of Spr. cornerstone	10x15 cm. glass plate	159
2288detail	Pageant-Congress Park	8x10 glass plate	161
2247	Pageant-Rev. War 1913	5x7 glass plate	161
2250	Pageant-Maize dance	5x7 glass plate	162
960	Masons	8x10 glass plate	164
1132	Comedy Club	8x10 glass plate	164
11.841	WGY Home Paper	4x5 safety film	165
3047	Todd Valentine party	8x10 glass plate	166
2776	Corn Husking Bee	8x10 glass plate	167
10.096/3	Jack's Harlem Club	4x5 safety film	167
7837/1	Wagon Wheel	8x10 cell. nitrate	168
8372detail	Span.-Amer. War Vets.	8x10 cell. nitrate	168
1093	Coon Club	8x10 glass plate	170
11.296/4	McGregor Golf Club	4x5 safety film	171
2039/1	Saratoga Winter Club	5x7 glass plate	171
4905	Co. L. Baseball team	8x10 cell. nitrate	172
5733	Jewish Athletic Club	8x10 cell. nitrate	173

6006detail	"Jockey Y"	8x10 cell. nitrate	180
9803/17	Steeplechase	4x5 safety film	182
9003/15	Pari-Mutual windows	4x5 safety film	184
2914	Original ATC ext.	5x7 glass plate	188

STODDARD, Seneca Ray
70-109	D & H Depot 1887	4x5 copy negative	45

WOOLEY, Jesse S.
W66	Broadway opp US Hotel	5x7 glass plate	6 and 60
W10	Post Office interior	5x7 glass plate	29
W89	Convention Hall ext.	5x7 glass plate	33
W81A	Town Hall	5x7 glass plate	41
W95	United States Hotel	5x7 glass plate	60
W11	Congress Hall	5x7 glass plate	66
W92	First Baptist Church	5x7 glass plate	90
W21	St. Peter's Church	5x7 glass plate	91
W132	Clark Textile Mill	9x15 cm. cell. nit.	107
W112	Yaddo mansion	9x15 cm. cell. nit.	121
83-87	Old vets/Broadway	4x5 copy negative	133
W25	Broadway Saratoga	5x7 glass plate	138
W85	Newman's Lake House	5x7 glass plate	148
74-101	YMCA fund raising	5x7 glass plate	172

UNKNOWN PHOTOGRAPHERS
S34	Congress Spg. Pav.	3 1/4x4 1/2 glass	cover
9945/A	Broadway-oldest image	4x5 copy neg	10
80-113	Star Spring	4x5 copy neg	13
80-09/6	Washington Spring	4x5 copy neg.	14
71-103	Broadway-GAR arch	4x5 copy neg	15
72-67/8	C. C. Cook	4x5 copy neg	17
58-239/b	Settle-37 Putnam St.	4x5 glass plate	21
50-257/5	Acme News	4x5 safety film	23
65-157	Police	4x5 copy neg	29
57-49	Police-with flags	4x5 copy neg	30
71.117/2	Arcade fire	4x5 copy neg	31
69-60/1	Fire House/Broadway	4x5 copy neg	31
80-138	FDR and Eleanor	4x5 copy neg	35
73-24	Officals of Saratoga Spg.	4x5 copy neg	39
80-62/2	Desjardins Blacksmith	4x5 copy neg	42
72-50	Hackman's Asson.	4x5 copy neg	44
82-91	D & H Depot construct.	4x5 copy neg	46
63-118/4	Grant's funeral train	4x5 copy neg	47
76-112	Trolley platform	4x5 copy neg	48
9805/C	Double decker trolley	4x5 copy neg	49
81-24	Hudson Valley Motor Co.	4x5 copy neg	50
72-70	Am. Express	4x5 copy neg	52
12.602	Monty Woolley birthday	4x5 copy neg	57
74-165	Movie clip-Saratoga	half frame 35mm nit	62
55-283	Grand Central Hotel	4x5 copy neg	63
S-30	Windsor Hotel	3 1/4x4 1/2 glass	65
S-26	Windsor Parlor	3 1/4x4 1/2 glass	66
78-21/2	Congress Hall Piazza	4x5 copy neg	66
72-73	J. F. Hasenfuss Cafe	4x5 copy neg	68
79-75	Sweeny's Hotel	4x5 copy neg	69
75-128/4	Geo. S. Batcheller	4x5 copy neg	79

I N D E X

BEVERLEY MASTRIANNI is a sculptor who lives and works in Saratoga Springs, where she attended Skidmore College and where she lives today with her husband Sam, a physician. In the early 1980s she founded and directed the Ann Grey Gallery, a gallery of regional contemporary art, for the Historical Society of Saratoga Springs. One of the exhibits in the gallery was called "The Saratoga Album" which featured photographs from the George S. Bolster Collection and by George Bolster. She later began working with Mr. Bolster to catalog his collection of thousands of photographic images of Saratoga Springs and to record the stories and information that he had collected during his lifetime. As well as coordinating this book, Mrs. Mastrianni researched the photographs and wrote the captions.

MICHAEL L. NOONAN is a Saratoga Springs native who met George Bolster in the late 1960s and spent eighteen years working as Mr. Bolster's apprentice and assistant. A skilled photographer with an intimate knowledge of the George S. Bolster Collection and its history, Mr. Noonan served as photographic archivist and printer for this book. His work with Mrs. Mastrianni and the Historical Society of Saratoga Springs to preserve the collection continues. Mr. Noonan lives in Saratoga Springs with his wife Kristin, an artist.

CHRIS CAROLA is a journalist and former feature writer and sports editor of the Saratogian newspaper in Saratoga Springs. A native of Mechanicville, in New York's Saratoga County, Mr. Carola moved to Saratoga Springs in 1985, where he lives with his wife Kathleen. Mr. Carola, who has written several articles on photographic collections, wrote the text for this book, his first.